MORE OVERHEARD IN DUBLIN

DUBLIN WIT FROM OVERHEARDINDUBLIN.COM

Gill & Macmillan

For Sophie

Gill & Macmillan Ltd
Hume Avenue, Park West, Dublin 12
with associated companies throughout the world
www.gillmacmillan.ie
© Gerard Kelly and Sinéad Kelly 2008
978 07171 45430

Print origination by TypeIT, Dublin
Illustrations by Eoin Coveney
Printed and bound by Norhaven A/S,
Denmark

This book is typeset in (typeface & size) on (leading).

The paper used in this book comes from the wood pulp
of managed forests. For every tree felled, at least one
tree is planted, thereby renewing natural resources.

A CIP catalogue record for this book is available from
the British Library.

5 4 3 2 1

Your tube

I was standing at the bus stop this morning, and two elderly men were having a chat. I overheard one say to the other, 'I had the tube down my throat — hope it wasn't the same tube you had up your arse!'

I had to turn away so they wouldn't see me laughing ...

Overheard by Darren, Inchicore
Posted on Friday, 14 March 2008

I love Parmesan cheese

Enjoying a meal in Flanagan's restaurant on O'Connell Street. At the table beside me were a young Dublin 'howya' couple out for a special night. The girl had ordered a bowl of spaghetti.

As the waiter was passing by, the young Dub girl pipes up, 'Hey, Mister, ya don't have any of dat Palmerstown cheese for me pasta, d'ya, love?'

Overheard by SJ, Flanagan's restaurant, O'Connell Street
Posted on Friday, 14 March 2008

Cluedo on the Nitelink

I was on the Nitelink coming home from town when two lads in their thirties stood up to get off at Dundrum. One of them was wearing a pair of yellow trousers. Some Head-the-Ball down the back of the bus shouts out,

'Colonel Mustard, in the billiard room, with the trousers!'

Yer man wasn't impressed!

Overheard by locko, Nitelink, Dundrum
Posted on Thursday, 13 March 2008

Caught doing a 'Martin Cahill'

On the Luas last week, three skangers bunk on at Inchicore bridge and only travel two stops. They spotted two gardaí walking along the footpath across the road. One of the youths replicates the hand-over-the-face gesture that was made famous by the late Martin Cahill, aka The General.

One of the gardaí spotted this and returns the gesture back to the youth.

If this wasn't funny enough, the youth then says, 'I'm gonna text Johnor te tell him wah happened.'

Just as they were getting off, he turns and asks his mate, 'How de ye spell "caught"?'

His mate replied, 'C–O–T, ya f**ken doughnut!'

Overheard by Danny, Luas
Posted on Thursday, 13 March 2008

Mahon Tribunal issues statement

Seen rather than heard.

Written on a T-shirt in Temple Bar:

> Been there
>
> Done that
>
> Bought the Taoiseach

Overheard by K, seen on a T-shirt in Temple Bar
Posted on Wednesday, 12 March 2008

Motion over the ocean

I was recently on a very turbulent flight from Tenerife to Dublin and was feeling out of control and nervous. Five or ten minutes into this turbulence, two lads in their forties, who looked like they liked their booze, began to sing:

'Oh, I'd like to know where you got the motion, rock the boat, don't rock the boat, baby!'

And of course the rest off the plane joined in, which then made me laugh and sweat like crazy and even more nervous.

Could only happen with a plane full of Dubliners on the way to Dublin!

Overheard by David, mid air over the Atlantic
Posted on Wednesday, 12 March 2008

Never been to Lesbinia!

On the no. 77 bus coming home from work during the summer, there was a large group of female Spanish students. As the bus travelled along the route, the group got smaller and smaller as each got off at their respective stops.

As one girl was saying goodbye to her friend, she turned and kissed her on the cheek. In front of me, a Cork culchie (obviously only in Dublin for the day!) turns to his mate and asks, 'Are they lesbians?'

Without even batting an eyelid, or turning his head, the other culchie replies, deadpan,

'No — they're Spanish!'

I nearly folded!

Overheard by Arty, on the mighty no. 77 bus!
Posted on Tuesday, 11 March 2008

Genital chips

Standing in the local chipper waiting for my food. Guy in front of me is waiting for his bag of chips.

Guy behind the counter gets his chips and asks him, 'Would you like salt and vinegar?'

Guy waiting on chips replies, 'Yeah, salt the bollix out of them.'

Overheard by Dubliner, local chipper
Posted on Monday, 10 March 2008

Work benefits

Overheard in Tesco, mother to young son:

'I am *not* payin' €4 for Sellotape when I have some in work!'

Overheard by Elaine, Tesco, Bray
Posted on Saturday, 8 March 2008

'Show me the money!' Gerry Maguire

Text to friend last week:

'Pint? I'm meeting some of the lads in Doyle's at nine. Hope you can make it.'

Instant reply from mate:

'You had me at "pint".'

Overheard by Paulo, by text
Posted on Sunday, 9 March 2008

Overheard incorrectly in Dublin

It was my first week working in a supermarket during the school holidays and I was busy packing shelves. An old lady asked me for the jacks, so I brought her to the ladies and said I'd wait outside. She looked puzzled and asked me why I brought her there. I said, 'It's because you asked for the bathroom ...'

She said, 'I'm looking for AJAX!'

I still cringe every time I think of it!

Overheard by Breda, SuperValu, Killester
Posted on Friday, 7 March 2008

Outta his head

I was out in town one night when three heads walk by, one of them far more drunk than his two mates who were propping him up in the middle.

Suddenly he pipes up loudly: 'Here, lads, come on and we'll go to the George for a dance, wha?'

His mates clearly embarrassed: 'No, Mick, we're heading home, come on.'

Two mates whisper over the top of his head to each other: 'F**k sake, if he could hear himself!'

Mick: 'F**k sake, man, what's the harm in havin' a dance to a bit of Kylie? Good music that is!'

Friend: 'Jaysus, his Ma was right — wine and beer do make him feel queer!'

Overheard by Niamh, Temple Bar
Posted on Tuesday, 4 March 2008

Androgynous rocker

While practising for a gig, the next band had a very feminine, long-haired rocker type waiting for his turn to play. One of the girls who was hanging around pipes up: 'Do you ever get mistaken for a girl?'

His quick-witted reply: 'No, do you?'

Overheard by yamadyoke, community centre
Posted on Tuesday, 4 March 2008

You're in Dublin now

Was over from England last weekend visiting family. We were sitting on the Airlink bus when a crowd of foreigners got on, dumped their luggage and stood next to the luggage racks. Inspector gets on and says, 'Youse lot go and sit upstairs, your bags are perfectly safe, you're in Dublin now!'

Overheard by Tommy, Dublin Airport
Posted on Monday, 3 March 2008

How to fail an eyesight exam in spectacular style

My sister recently had to go for a medical for work. During the eye test she was asked to look into this machine and call out the last line on the screen, so she started calling out, 'a ... g ... h ... pass ... pass ... r'.

Then the doctor asked her to call out the next line up from that one. She called out, 'd ... t ... e ... f ... n ...', slightly happier with herself for her ability to read this line.

She had struggled on one or two on the last line so she knew the doctor wouldn't exactly praise her sight, but nothing could have prepared her for the doctor's comments:

'Madam, I'm afraid we will have to investigate your eye sight in more detail — there were no letters on that screen — they were all numbers ...'

Overheard by Anonymous, from my sister
Posted on Thursday, 28 February 2008

The different stages of drunkenness ...

Two blokes who passed me by on Nassau Street gave me a whole new insight into classifications of inebriation.

First Guy: 'I can't believe you said that to her!'

Second Guy: 'I know man, I know!'

First Guy: 'Were you drunk or what?'

Second Guy (thinks for a second): 'Well ... not "drunk" drunk. Just sort of "shite at pool" drunk.'

Overheard by Ella, outside the Spar on Nassau Street
Posted on Tuesday, 26 February 2008

IT genius

During my retirement, I offered to help out one day in a PLC college, teaching IT technology.

I hear a growl of annoyance from a young female, who cannot sign into her messenger.

She troubleshoots and then shouts,

'It says der's sumting wrong with me poxy service!'

(proxy server!)

Overheard by Don, PLC college
Posted on Tuesday, 26 February 2008

Not a leg to stand on

I recently brought my uncle, who is in his late 70s, to his local doctor, as he was complaining of numbness and loss of feeling in his right leg.

My uncle, who has been a heavy smoker all of his life, was becoming a regular visitor to the surgery and knew the doctor on a personal basis.

Doctor: 'Well, Tony, what's the problem?'

Tony: 'It's this bloody leg of mine, I can't walk very far without my leg becoming numb and dead.'

Doctor: 'Well Tony, it's a combination of smoking and old age, these things happen as we grow older.'

Tony: 'Old age?'

Doctor: 'Yes, Tony, do you understand?'

Tony: 'Not really. The left leg is the same age and I have no problem with that one ...'

Overheard by Higgs, local GP, Kimmage
Posted on Tuesday, 19 February 2008

Digital milk?

I used to work in a newsagents, and Avonmore were doing a promotion for digital cameras where you collected tokens from milk cartons. One customer comes over to me and asks,

'What's the difference between digital milk and low fat milk?'

Overheard by Anonymous, Finglas
Posted on Monday, 18 February 2008

Gender confusion!

Shopping in town, I passed two women talking on the street. One of them had a baby with her.

Woman #1 (with baby): 'Have ya met me little grandson?'

Woman #2 (peers down at baby): 'Ah lovely — is it a boy or a girl?'

Overheard by Aisling, in town
Posted on Monday, 18 February 2008

Happy Valliers!

I was sitting waiting for the bus to move off from my stop the other day. The entire bus was pretty quiet apart from the hum of the driver's radio. Suddenly, the local 'Anto' gets on and livens the whole place up with this phone conversation:

Anto: 'Howya, €2 please, cheers!'

Anto (on phone): 'Sorry der, love, wha were ya sayin?'

Anto (in a shocked voice): 'WHA?! A DIVORCE?! WHA ... WHY?! Hell ... hello? hello?'

Anto marches off the bus muttering to himself: 'Great, now I have to learn how to wash, cook, clean ...'

Although we felt sorry for him, the entire bus (including the driver) CRACKED up laughing.

Overheard by Thomas, bus terminus
Posted on Monday, 18 February 2008

Where there's a will there's a way

My friend, who is a diabetic, is doing a 48-hour fast for charity. I asked her how she manages, when diabetics are supposed to eat something every few hours. 'That's easy,' she said, 'I just do it in three-hour stretches!'

Overheard by Anonymous, from a friend in Walkinstown
Posted on Saturday, 16 February 2008

Communication breakdown

I guess we just take our rights for granted ...

Walking through Dunnes in town I see an Asian girl carefully stacking the shelves. A young Irish manager walks confusedly up to her and asks her why she's still working.

She mumbles an answer, to which the manager replies, 'No, no, that's just my sense of humour, I was only joking when I said you didn't work hard enough for a lunchbreak!'

Overheard by Lindy, Dunnes, Georges Street
Posted on Friday, 15 February 2008

Stinger

A couple of years ago, a friend of mine, about 20 at the time, stumbled out of the Big Tree pub one night onto Dorset Street. Totally pissed drunk with some random bird on his arm, he hailed a taxi. Both of them jump in the back and my mate says, 'Beaumont please.'

The taxi driver replies, 'I know where you f**kin' live Tomas!'

My mate: 'Oh ... sorry, Dad!'

Overheard by Stephen, taxi
Posted on Sunday, 13 January 2008

Homicidal seats

On the bus, sitting on the top deck.

Drunk woman stands up to get off and walks into a seat. She shouts at the seat, 'Ya dirty whore, what'd ya hit me for?!'

Failing to receive an answer, she turns away still shouting — and falls down the stairs! Only in Dublin!

Overheard by flyingcabbage, on the top deck of a bus
Posted on Monday, 11 February 2008

Terminate-her!

I am an Austrian guy, tall and quite a big build. Was in the Oliver St John Gogarty's celebrating New Year's Eve with my Irish girlfriend and some friends. It was packed as usual with the normal mixture of Irish and tourists.

Went to the bar to order some drinks. An English girl standing beside me who obviously overheard my accent turned, and the conversation went something like this:

Girl: 'Oh, you must be American?'

Me: 'No, actually, I'm Austrian.'

Girl: 'Wow, really? I could've sworn you were American, you sound exactly like Arnold Schwarzenegger.'

Overheard by Alexander, Oliver St John Gogarty, Temple Bar
Posted on Friday, 8 February 2008

A slight exaggeration

Walking down Georges Street in Dublin, an elderly Dublin man with a stick stopped me and said, 'Here young fella, ya wouldn't help me across the road, me sight isn't the best.' I said no problem and walked the man across.

Half way there, he turned and said, 'Jaysis, thanks young fella, the last time I tried to cross the road I got flattened by a bus!'

Overheard by David, Georges Street, Dublin
Posted on Sunday, 3 February 2008

Irish Lessons

My friend Liam was in the company of a few native Irish speakers in a pub in Connemara recently when a discussion began about what the correct Irish terminology was for a variety of different sexual activities.

One of them then asked an old guy in the corner who was obviously eavesdropping on the conversation if he knew the correct Irish for cunnilingus.

Quick as a flash he comes back with, 'Níl mé in ann smaoineamh ar faoi láthair ach bhí sé ar barr mo theanga ar maidin.'

(I can't think of it now but it was on the tip of my tongue this morning.)

And they say Irish is a dead language!

Overheard by Tara, from my friend Liam in Dublin
Posted on Thursday, 31 January 2008

Sales meeting

My uncle Frank was talking to his manager about a sales meeting. The manager was trying to give him some wickedly insightful judgment about all involved.

The manager goes off on a rant that Frank was facetious, that it's fair to say the other people at the meeting were also facetious, that out of the four people there he himself was the only one who wasn't facetious.

To which Frank interjected with, 'Do you know what "facetious" means?'

Manager asks, 'Frank, do you think I am using words out of contents?'

Pure LEGEND!

Overheard by Ratzer, Starbucks, Dundrum
Posted on Thursday, 31 January 2008

Dirty burds

Heard this from the mother at the weekend. She had just got on a train at Heuston, and a hen party of the roughest-looking women you've ever seen (plus one blow-up doll called Roger wearing Y-fronts) came through the carriage, screeching and laughing and skulling cans of Satzenbrau.

Anyway, in the midst of all the merriment came this little gem:

'Heeyor! Whatcha mean ya need de tylet!? Sure I have a cup here ya can use — look!'

Overheard by Morticia, Heuston Station
Posted on Wednesday, 30 January 2008

Wakey majakey

I was at the recent Terenure v Belvedere match in Donnybrook. I then see this young wan in a Belvedere jersey chatting to her mate on the phone and she says in the biggest D4 accent,

'And the Terenure guy took down his trousers and waved his wakey-majakey at me!'

Me and my mates were in stitches!

Overheard by Tom, Terenure v Belvedere match, Donnybrook
Posted on Tuesday, 29 January 2008

Enough to make you sick!

Called in to see a friend in hospital the other day. She had no complaints with the service there, except for one thing:

'Long after I'm gone to sleep at night, around half eleven or quarter to twelve, some nurse wakes me up to give me a sleeping tablet!'

Overheard by Anonymous, in a Dublin hospital
Posted on Sunday, 27 January 2008

Toilet training Granny

Yesterday as I went into Dunnes, a child, mother and Granny came in behind me. It was pouring rain, and Granny said, 'Oh, my pants are all wet, I'm soaking.'

Little kid, aged about three, turns to Mammy and said,

'Oh no, Mammy, I think Granny had a little accident!'

Overheard by Anonymous, Dunnes Stores
Posted on Friday, 25 January 2008

The times are changing

Back in Ireland on holiday last summer, having lived abroad for many years, I was at a BBQ chatting with friends about how much Ireland has changed over the years.

One of my friends who lived abroad for as long as I had says, whilst looking at the barbeque, 'Be Jaysus, when I left Ireland we used to eat inside the house and shite outside. Now they f**king eat outside and shite inside!'

Overheard by Niall, at a BBQ
Posted on Thursday, 24 January 2008

Fancy name

I was sitting in a waiting room in hospital beside this man when an orderly walked in who knew him.

Orderly: 'Jaysus, Mick, how's it going? Haven't seen you in a while!'

Mick: 'Ah, not so bad now, not so bad.'

Orderly: 'C'mere, are ya still working with your man, what's his name?'

Mick: 'Who's that now?'

Orderly: 'Ah you know him, jaysus it's a fancy name, on the tip of me tongue it is, kinda foreign is it? He's about that height (gesturing with his hands), ah you know him, a real fancy name, could be foreign, start with a T or something does it?'

Mick (very hesitantly): 'Tom is it?'

Orderly: 'Ah Tom — that's it!'

Overheard by Niamh, St James's Hospital
Posted on Tuesday, 22 January 2008

Have some respect!

One day I got on the mighty no. 123 bus, when an older man around 70 starting pushing myself and the others onto the bus, saying, 'Come on will ya move up the bleeding bus.' After a few minutes I hear him shouting again from the top of the bus saying and pointing, 'You, Missus, are you getting off? Make way everyone, will you f**king move and let the woman through.'

At the next stop a guy gets on the bus, a totally normal guy carrying a bottle of 7Up, and the old guy starts yelling, 'Jayus! You can't bring that on the bus, have some f**king respect for the bus driver will ya,' and grabs the man's 7Up!

Then when he finally gets off the bus he looks at the bus driver and says, 'See ya soon boss,' and gives him a salute.

Think he thought he worked for Dublin Bus!

Overheard by Therese, no. 123 bus
Posted on Monday, 21 January 2008

The sad state of 'reality'

Girl: 'Did ya see *You're A Star* the other night?'

Guy: 'Nah, me Gran died so we didn't get a chance.'

Girl: 'Did ya vote for it though?'

Guy: 'Yeah, Granny was there dead in the bed an' we were all textin' over her ...'

Overheard by Anonymous, on the no. 16A bus
Posted on Monday, 21 January 2008

Too good for you

My Mam was on a no. 77 bus going home to Tallaght, when she heard a group of boys trying to chat up some girls about the same age (15 or 16) down the back of the bus.

As the girls got to get off the bus, one of the fellas asked for their phone number.

Stepping down the stairs one of the girls replied (very loudly), '085 22 2 good for u.'

Everyone was in stitches!

Overheard by Anonymous, bus to Tallaght
Posted on Monday, 21 January 2008

It's really just a mart for culchies

I was walking up Harcourt Street on Friday just after leaving work. Outside Coppers was some kind of sewerage truck with a long pipe going downstairs into the night club. One of the girls I was with says,

'Oh my god, are they sucking the shite out of Coppers?'

Overheard by Brian, Harcourt Street
Posted on Monday, 21 January 2008

Area code prejudice!

A woman was browsing in an expensive tile shop. She asked the sales assistant, 'How much does it cost to lay tiles?'

The assistant replied, 'Well, it depends on the area.' The woman asked, 'Oh, so if you lived in Ballsbridge, would it cost a lot more?'

Overheard by Anonymous, a tile shop on the south side
Posted on Tuesday, 15 January 2008

George Orwell would turn in his grave

I was in Eason's in O'Connell Street today, looking for George Orwell's *Animal Farm* for school. I couldn't find it in the school novels section so I asked the assistant where I might find it.

He looks at me blankly for about 15 seconds and

then says, 'Well, in Pet Care, over there, I suppose ...'

Right ...

Overheard by Anonymous, Eason's
Posted on Sunday, 13 January 2008

The no frills airline (really!)

On a Ryanair flight to Edinburgh a few weeks ago, the air hostess kept pausing during the safety demonstration.

'In the event of a drop in cabin pressure, oxygen masks will drop down. Pull mask down and place over your face.' Pauses. Young lad down the back shouts, '... and insert €2 for oxygen!'

The whole plane was in stitches —everyone except for the air hostess!

Overheard by Steven, on a Ryanair flight
Posted on Tuesday, 8 January 2008

Xmas cheer

I was in the Statoil garage in Cabra on Christmas Day when I overheard a young lad of about 15 talking to his mates about what his father had given him for Christmas.

Young Lad: '... me Da gave me €250 for Christmas ... I swear to God I nearly hugged him!'

Overheard by Mr.X, Statoil, New Cabra Road
Posted on Saturday, 5 January 2008

Shell suits to sea

In a packed off-licence, a young lad was standing in the queue in his finest white kappa tracksuit and a cardboard box full of cans in his arms. The bottom of the box gave way and his cans went everywhere, beer pissing out of half of them.

While he was deciding what to do with his jaw hanging down, a pissed aul' lad leans in and says, 'That's what you get for wearing a tracksuit!'

Overheard by Whelo, Malahide
Posted on Saturday, 5 January 2008

He got a right de-bollicking!

I work in a veterinary clinic and I answered a phone call one day:

Woman: 'I need to have my dog's stitches out.'

Me: 'Okay, what did your dog have done?'

Woman: 'Oh, what's this you'd call it ... I suppose he was de-bollickated. Is that what you'd say?'

Me: 'Well, I'd say neutered ...'

Overheard by Anonymous, veterinary clinic
Posted on Friday, 4 January 2008

The lunatics are running the asylum

My pal to a head of lettuce she was rinsing in the sink:

'Goin' anywhere nice on your holidays, love?'

Overheard by Anonymous, kitchen
Posted on Thursday, 3 January 2008

And they're off!

Some years back while walking down Baggot Street after an evening out, we were 10 yards behind a family of American tourists making their way back to their hotel. As they passed a bookies shop, one of the group pointed at the sign over the window and exclaimed,

'Hey! Look at that! "Baggot Racing"! What the hell's a Baggot?'

We had nearly recovered from laughing when 50 yards further on they passed a laundrette called 'Baggot Cleaners' and one says,

'Jeez, they must race them back there and then clean them in here ... We gotta come back and see this tomorrow ...'

Overheard by Pucfada, Baggot Street
Posted on Thursday, 27 December 2007

The concerned thief

I was awoken about 4.30 a.m. the other week by the sound of someone trying to break the lock on my side gate to steal my moped which was in the rear garden.

Rather than corner the bloke, I went around the front of the house and shouted at him as loud as I could, 'What the f**k do you think you're doing?'

The look on his face was priceless but he then climbed over the wall into my neighbour's garden and I continued shouting after him, at which point he stopped, turned around and said,

'Will ya shut da f**k up, yer gonna wake everyone up!'

Overheard by Fran, Firhouse
Posted on Thursday, 20 December 2007

Crazy dress code

A few years ago, I went to a fancy-dress party at a pub as a pint of Guinness. I was under a big cylinder covered in black bin liners, with my arms and legs sticking out. Had a cream collar and a harp on my chest.

I approached the door and the bouncer stopped me. He looked me — a pint of Guinness — up and down, and said deadpan,

'Sorry, pal, I can't let you in here wearing runners.'

Overheard by AG, Tara Street
Posted on Monday, 17 December 2007

No, the feathered two-legged type!

At a table quiz in work.

Quizmaster: 'Name the bird of peace.'

Random shout from a table: 'Mother Teresa!'

Overheard by Doots, work table quiz, The Vaults
Posted on Friday, 14 December 2007

Poor Mikey ain't getting time off?

Not so much heard as seen!

Was having a slash in the toilets at UCD and as I was washing my hands I noticed the check sheet which states when and who check the toilets to make sure they're clean, etc. Reading down I saw many signatures and dates when they were checked. One of the latest read:

Date: 11/12/07

Checked by: Mikey from Boyzone

Overheard by Shaggy, UCD
Posted on Tuesday, 11 December 2007

Plane logic

During the safety demonstration on board a Ryanair flight from Dublin to Leeds, there's two real Dubs sitting next to me. The cabin crew get to the bit about the life-jacket, and one fella turns to his mate and says:

'Why the f**k do they give ya a life-jacket on a plane, f**k sake, that's like given ya a bleeden parachute on a boat.'

Overheard by Steve, on a Ryanair flight from Dublin to Leeds
Posted on Saturday, 8 December 2007

Operation Freeflow my arse!

Garda at a set of lights in Drumcondra, directing traffic with one of those glow-sticks. Lights were green but the garda was directing our lane to stop. My brother drives straight on through the lights past the garda, and I pointed out that he was supposed to stop.

He replies,

'I'm not stopping for some fucking culchie with a light sabre.'

Overheard by Anonymous, Drumcondra
Posted on Thursday, 6 December 2007

A long time ago in a romper room far far away

Had brought my daughter to Play Zone in Celbridge, a kind of padded room for toddlers with ball pits, climbing frames, slides etc. Heard another father trying to coax his son into sliding down one of those enclosed, tube-like slides.

Son looks into the dark hole at the top of the slide and goes to Dad, 'But I don't want to go down the dark slide.'

Dad thinks about it then goes, 'Only by conquering your fears can you ever hope to defeat the dark slide.'

Son still wouldn't slide down it!

Overheard by Bet Down Dad, Play Zone in Celbridge
Posted on Tuesday, 4 December 2007

Who am I?

Well, what you have to know first to understand the story is the fact that I have naturally blonde hair and blue eyes. For years I've had people mistaken me for being from Sweden and over-pronouncing words thinking I can't understand their English (even though I've been born and reared in Dublin!).

Yesterday while shopping I was waiting for my sister so I sat down on a bench and a real 'aul' one' sat down beside me.

This conversation actually happened:

Old Woman: 'If you don't mind me asking, love, what country are you from?'

Me: 'Ha! No, I'm Irish, I'm from Dublin.'

Old Woman: 'Oh jaysus, sorry, love.'

Me: 'It's grand. I actually get that a lot ...'

Old Woman: 'I'd say ye do, love. Ya look Swedish or Dutch or somewhere far away like that. Are sure you're from Ireland, pet?'

Me: 'Yeah!'

Old Woman (while getting up to leave): 'I'd check your birth cert if I were you ...'

Overheard by Kimberly, The Square, Tallaght
Posted on Thursday, 29 November 2007

Forgiven and forgotten

My cousin was talking with two friends at the front door about her son's waster of a father:

'Ah, but ya gave birth to lovely kids considerin' ...'

'I have a very forgivin' fanny!'

Overheard by bobby, Clondalkin
Posted on Monday, 26 November 2007

Kitty

A few weeks ago we were sitting watching TV in the living-room. There was myself, me Da, Ma and brother. Suddenly the cat walked into the room with a €5 note in its mouth (obviously dropped by somebody because I don't think the cat's working yet). Then me Da comes out with a classic:

'Who put the fiver in the kitty?'

Brilliant!

Overheard by Fred Flintstone, Ballyfermot
Posted on Sunday, 25 November 2007

Getting what you can

A few years ago when I was in sixth year there was a panto going on. In the changing rooms during the interval I overheard two first-year lads about 12 years old talking about other first-year girls. One delivered this killer line:

Lad: 'Shut up, Gav, you're gay! You went out with yer one Aine for two months and got nothing off her!'

Gav: 'So?'

Lad: 'I went out with her younger sister, and got CDs!'

Overheard by Charlie, panto changing rooms, school
Posted on Sunday, 18 November 2007

Just blame it on the aul' wans

Was standing in UCD waiting for a no. 17 bus. One of those new 07 buses pulls in with no one on it. The front left-hand side of the bus smashes into the kerb, the driver hops out, examines the damage, lights up a smoke, glances at me and says,

'F**k it, sum aul' wan reversed inta me,' and walked on!

Overheard by Jonny, UCD
Posted on Sunday, 18 November 2007

Horny Harney

Myself and my wife were watching the news. An interview with the Minister for Health was followed by one about children sharing pornographic images on mobile phones and via websites like Bebo.

Thinking she would spare herself from the usual questions ('What's pornography' etc.), my wife asked our seven-year-old daughter to get something upstairs.

A couple of minutes later she re-entered the room behind us and declared, 'I'm horny!'

Stunned, we turned around to find her wearing a black wig and a smile, repeating, 'I'm Mary Horny!'

Overheard by Macker, our sitting-room
Posted on Sunday, 18 November 2007

Miss Guided?

Having presented some junior Girl Guides with their badges etc. at an investiture ceremony, the Guide leader was really warming to her theme. When it came to the award for the most senior of the girls, the leader gushed,

'... and not only is she great at taking care of the Girl Guides, she's well known for looking after the Boy Scouts around the village!'

Overheard by Anonymous, Guides investiture in Cabinteely
Posted on Sunday, 18 November 2007

Boneless

Arrived at the butcher's first thing one morning, to find him roaring laughing at a note some woman had shoved under his door.

It said, 'Paddy, please take the bone out of my leg!'

Overheard by Anonymous, Duffy's butchers shop, Clondalkin
Posted on Friday, 16 November 2007

Cringe TV

Watching RTÉ the other night about new apartments in Ratoath being developed so that everyone with any disability can live there, hassle free etc. They were giving disabled people a tour of the apartments and the foreman walks into one of the apartments with a blind girl and her guide dog.

First thing he says to her: 'As you can see, the lights come on automatically.'

Silence from the blind girl ...!

Only on Irish TV!

Overheard by Anonymous, Blesso
Posted on Friday, 16 November 2007

That should narrow it down

At a recent wedding a friend who was seated at our table went out to the hotel foyer where she encountered a small boy, also a wedding guest, crying while sitting on the stairs. She asked why he was crying and he said he had lost his Mammy.

'Okay, no problem,' she says, 'what's her name?'

'MAAMMMMY,' replied the boy.

Overheard by lenny, at a wedding in Dublin
Posted on Thursday, 15 November 2007

Foreign nationals need Dublin Bus to lead them to their Promised Land!

Just yesterday, whilst RTÉ *Drivetime* were interviewing people in Finglas regarding the effects of the Dublin Bus dispute, one lady was concerned about 'the foreigners'. She said, 'Sure they don't know their way around, how will they get to their destiny?'

Overheard by Anonymous, RTÉ *Drivetime*, 12 November 2007
Posted on Tuesday, 13 November 2007

F word

Being a teacher, I hear some strange stories from students but this one tops them all. The girls had a different teacher for sex education last year, and one of my 10 year olds came back mortified:

'Miss, ya'd never guess wha da teacher sed! She sed da F word!'

Worried at what this word might be, I told her to tell me later. At the end of the day I asked her what this F word was.

'Ah, Miss, ya wouldn't believe it ... da teacher said FANGINA!'

Overheard by miss c, school in Dublin 12
Posted on Monday, 12 November 2007

John Player euxxx!

Couple of years ago at a party with a bunch of mates, we ran out of smokes. So wandered up to this chubby middle-aged woman I hadn't met before, smoking, and politely asked, 'Wouldn't have a spare smoke, would ya, please?'

Her response, deadpan, deadly serious with glazed eyes: 'Give us a lick out, would yeh?'

I bought some instead ...

Overheard by Eamo, the Noggin Inn
Posted on Monday, 12 November 2007

Cats stuck together?

Walking down Grafton Street with two D4 type girls in front of me: 'So, are Siamese cats, loike, stuck together?'

Overheard by Bekah, Grafton Street
Posted on Sunday, 11 November 2007

Lessons in Irish

I live in Germany and was talking to a friend who had just returned from three years of working as a translator in Dublin. During the conversation she mentioned that she'd learned some Irish while she was over there, then rattled off the numbers one to ten, just to prove it.

I asked her how she got interested in Irish. 'Well, the Irish drop so many Irish words into English that I had to keep asking people what they meant,' she replied. 'After that it was just the same as learning any other language. You watch what people do and listen to what they say.'

I asked her for an example 'Well, when someone opens the door and sees the weather outside, listening to them taught me how to say, "It's raining" in Irish.'

After checking to make sure I could remember how to say it myself, I said, 'Go on then, how do you say it?' Without batting an eyelid she says, 'Aah for f**k sake!'

Overheard by Gapper, by my friend
Posted on Saturday, 10 November 2007

Toilet humour

I work on a building site near Heuston Station. The toilets are forever getting new literature on the walls, getting painted over, before new material appears. I saw a new one recently saying 'Polish workers — GO HOME'! The next day, below this some one had added, 'But leave your women'. The next day someone else had come in and scribbled '... and take ours with you!'

Overheard by Neil, construction site, Kilmainham
Posted on Saturday, 10 November 2007

An odie?

A fat bloke came into work yesterday to collect an order he had previously made. My young colleague went out back to the warehouse to get the bloke's order. He was gone some time and then eventually emerged with it and said to the fat bloke, 'I'm terribly sorry about the wait.'

To which the fat bloke replied, 'Don't worry, son, it's not your fault, I eat too much!'

Overheard by Anonymous, work
Posted on Thursday, 8 November 2007

Learning from Dad

Little girl on the bus, after spotting a fly (roaring): 'Look, Dad, a bastard!'

Overheard by Anonymous, on the bus
Posted on Thursday, 8 November 2007

Russia versus Ireland

My Dad overheard this on his coffee break in work.

Russian Guy: 'In Russia, only women put milk in their tea.'

Smart Ass Dub: 'Well, in Ireland only women drink vodka!'

Overheard by Traykool, from my Dad
· Posted on Monday, 5 November 2007

Nice one Grandad!

Kid: 'Grandad, how long is a minute?'

Grandad: 'Depends on which side of the toilet door you're standing.'

Overheard by Anonymous, half-time in Croke Park
Posted on Sunday, 4 November 2007

Forgetting the wife

An elderly man and lady were getting ready to get off the bus. When the bus pulled in to the stop, the man got off but the lady didn't.

When the bus began to pull away again the man ran after the bus and began banging on the window. The bus driver stopped and let him on the bus, with the man shouting: 'I forgot my wife!!'

Overheard by Greg, 46A
Posted on Monday, 5 November 2007

Dublin's future

I was walking through the Liberties with a little three year old I was minding. She had no buggy with her, and half way to where we were going

she sat down on the side of the road, with her hands on her face.

When I asked her what she was doing she looked up at me and said, 'Sitting!'

I asked why. She replied, 'Cause I'm f**kin' bollixed!'

Now, that's Dublin!

Overheard by Conor, outside Kevin Street Garda Station
Posted on Friday, 2 November 2007

Flat bus

Was waiting around for my bus yesterday evening when a lad comes up to me and asks, 'Has the braless bus gone yet?'

I was like 'What ...?' And he asks me again, 'Has the BRALESS bus gone yet?' I was like, 'Sorry, I don't know what you're talking about,' and he asks,

'For fook's sake, the bleedin' no. 32A bus, love, has it gone yet or wha?'

Took me a few minutes to work out what he meant!

Overheard by Chloe, no. 32A bus stop
Posted on Wednesday, 31 October 2007

Getting 'felt'

Many years ago I worked in a large hardware store in Capel Street. One day a lady walked into the store and enquired of the young sssistant at one of the counters, 'Excuse me, young man, can you tell me where I can get felt?'

He replied with a smirk on his face, 'In the basement, Madam.'

The lady took offence, called him rude and insolent and asked to speak with the manager, who politely informed her that yes, she could get felt in the basement!

We laughed about this for days!

Overheard by angie, Lenehans in Capel Street
Posted on Monday, 29 October 2007

The Dublin divide

Skanger: 'Ten Silk Cut Purple, please.'

Posh Assistant: 'Em, don't ya mean John Player Blue?'

Skanger: 'Give me the box of Silk Cut or I'll box ye in the face.'

Posh Assistant: 'OK ...'

Overheard by LongMileRoad, town
Posted on Saturday, 27 October 2007

Now there's a compliment

'What's wrong with you today? You've a head like a burst couch.'

Overheard by Anonymous, at home
Posted on Saturday, 27 October 2007

Can't get no satisfaction

Was queuing outside Coppers last night and ahead of me were two girls from Dublin who were very skangery (if that's a word). They were clearly over 21 but the bouncer was looking for an excuse not to let them in.

Bouncer: 'Sorry, girls, but if you don't have ID, I can't let you in.'

Girl: 'But I'm 26 for f**k sake.'

Bouncer: 'I don't care how old you are. I need to see ID to satisfy myself that you are old enough.'

Girl: 'I'd say you have to satisfy yourself full stop — ya ugly pig!'

Overheard by Len, outside Copper Face Jacks
Posted on Friday, 26 October 2007

All-Ireland Final day

After the 2006 All-Ireland Football Final (Mayo v Kerry) which Kerry won. Two Mayo women were walking through a residential street when they were approached by two local girls (about six and eight years old). The little girls got in their faces and started chanting 'You're shit! And you know you are. You're shit! And ...'

The Mayo women found this funny and started trying to reason with the girls saying, 'Ah come on now, we beat you in the semis,' but the girls were having none of it and began chanting 'Hill 16 is Dublin only, Hill 16 is Dublin only. Who are ya? Who are ya?'

At this point the girls' father strolled out of his front door. Realising what was going on, he clapped his hands together and roared over at the top of his voice, 'Hill 16 is Dublin only, Hill 16 is Dublin only.'

Overheard by Niall, outside Croke Park
Posted on Thursday, 25 October 2007

Stick it where?

Was with my Granny (about 70 years old, very Catholic, never curses) and two nephews in the park on Sunday. We got talking about how many young girls have kids but the kids' Dads are not around.

We both agreed that the men have it a lot easier in that situation, when my Gran said to me, 'Sure, they're just a randy lot — they would stick it in a keyhole if they could.'

Overheard by Pixi-b, Marley Park
Posted on Thursday, 25 October 2007

Numeracy building site style

Walking past a building site today and two foreign lads were filling a skip. They had a large 8x4 slab of wood between them.

One turns to the other and says, 'We go on 2. 1—2—3, OK, go!'

Overheard by Phanom-Anom, Dublin town
Posted on Thursday, 25 October 2007

Bodes well for the future

Was dropping the little lad into the crèche this

morning. After making sure he was okay, I said to him, 'You be a good boy for Sarah today.'

To which he replied, 'Don't worry, Daddy I won't be a little bollix like David over there!'

My lad is three!

Overheard by Santos L Helper, local crèche
Posted on Monday, 22 October 2007

The beer-bellied revolutionary

On returning from a Che Guevara 40th anniversary do, one of the regulars walked into the pub wearing a Che T-shirt. It was about three sizes too small and was stretched tight over his massive beer belly.

The barman took one look at him and shouts over, 'Jayses, Paul, I never knew Che's head was that big!'

Overheard by Anonymous, Celt Bar, Talbot Street
Posted on Saturday, 20 October 2007

The honest taxi driver

I was coming home from town in a taxi the night of the Junior Cert results in September. While chatting to the taxi driver he was telling me about how shocked he was at how well his daughter did.

'Well, she certainly didn't get the brains from me ... The milkman must've been a clever f****r!'

Overheard by Sean, back of a taxi
Posted on Saturday, 20 October 2007

The scholar

My friend bashed his head last week and got ambulanced off to Blanch. He's 69 years old, and studying as a mature student in NUIM. The ambulance fellas who brought him in told me that when they revived him after his accident (he was unconscious for 15 minutes) they asked him his name and what he did.

When he said he was a student, they thought the bash on the head had really done some serious damage. It took him quite a while to convince them he hadn't lost it altogether!

Overheard by Rudy, James Connolly Memorial Hospital
Posted on Friday, 19 October 2007

When you still think your passengers are kids

Three of us take turns driving into work. One morning we were getting picked up by Libby (who is a mother of three young children). On the way to work she must have forgotten who was in the car with her, because she suddenly pipes up in an overly excited voice, 'Ohhhhhhhhhhh wow, look at all the diggers over there,' thinking she had her kids in the car!

Overheard by Fiona, in a car on the way to work
Posted on Friday, 19 October 2007

Blooming brilliant!

Working in a florist, my manager was thinking of a poster to put in the window to grab people's attention. She told me she had a great idea and the next day she came in with the poster.

It was a big picture of a cactus and below it, 'NOT YOUR USUAL BUNCH OF PRICKS'!

Overheard by Daisy, work
Posted on Friday, 19 October 2007

First-time caller, long-time idiot

Message left on my mobile:

'James? ... JAMES, pick up ... I know you can hear me ... pick up the phone.'

Overheard by James, on my mobile
Posted on Friday, 19 October 2007

Foot & Mouth, or foot in mouth?

My sisters in-law from Wales were travelling over to Dublin by car ferry. It was at the time of the Foot & Mouth outbreak in the UK and Irish authorities were on high alert, spraying down all cars and asking passengers if they'd been on farms etc.

Disembarking in Dublin Port their car was stopped by an official. 'Any dairy products?' he asked, to which the driver replied in complete seriousness, 'No thanks, we're staying in a hotel and breakfast is included.'

The rest of the car erupted in laughter — still to the confusion of the driver!

Overheard by Gar, Dublin Port
Posted on Thursday, 18 October 2007

42

Say cheese

Was in the All Sports Café and there was a couple sitting at the next table. The waitress brought down two cocktails to them and left. The fella said to his girlfriend, 'We should have got a pitcher', to which she responds, 'But we don't even have a camera?!'

Overheard by Stroker, Temple Bar
Posted on Thursday, 18 October 2007

Claustrophobic holiday

An American tourist couple sitting on a park bench. The lady says to her husband, 'Don't you just get so claustrophobic in these small countries?'

Overheard by Paul, St Stephen's Green
Posted on Wednesday, 17 October 2007

Sap

Was walking past the newsagents when I see a young father of 25 reprimand his son of about seven who was attempting to follow his mother into the shop. I overheard this brief conversation:

Father: 'Yer not goin' in there, yer waitin' ouhh here wih meee!'

Son: 'Whyyyyyy?'

Father: 'Ya know why, I told ya why a minute ago why, what did I tell ya? Why can't ya go into the shop wih yer Mammy?'

Son (hangs head): 'Cos I was acting the f**kin' sap.'

Father: 'Exactly, ye were actin' the f**kin' sap.'

Overheard by cactus, Summerhill
Posted on Wednesday, 17 October 2007

Irish Rail, having a laugh

Public Address: 'We wish to apologise for the late boarding of the 07:30 hours service to Waterford. Boarding will commence in approximately 10 minutes.'

Irish Rail staff on the platform: '10 minutes!' — and then raucous laughter!

Overheard by Anonymous, Heuston Station
Posted on Wednesday, 17 October 2007

Service with a smile?

At the Police concert, ordering a hot dog.

I asked the woman serving,

'Could I have some onions on the hot dog?'

Her reply, 'Where the f**k do you think you are, America?'

Classy!

Overheard by Little Larry, Croke Park
Posted on Wednesday, 17 October 2007

A city of contrasts

Last August I was in Dublin for a couple of nights with a friend, staying in Buswells. One night we decided to take a taxi to the Omniplex, and discovered the driver lived on the southside but

44

was from Wicklow originally (you know the way taxi drivers have that amazing talent of telling their entire life story in less than five minutes).

Realising he has a pair of culchies with him, he started on about how Dublin isn't half as bad as the media make out, and how in all his 20 years of living here he's never been robbed or had any sort of trouble and that we were as safe here as we would be back in our little village.

All very well and good, two hours later we were getting a taxi back. Driver was a northsider this time, took a different route back to the hotel. Driving down a narrow street with feck all light and quite a bit of graffiti, he announces, 'Hauld on to yer handbags, ladies, this is where da druggies hang out.'

Overheard by Effy, taxi ride from the Omniplex to Buswells Hotel

Posted on Wednesday, 17 October 2007

Hopes and dreams

Years back in primary school the teacher asks, 'What would you like to be when you grow up?'

Student #1: 'Policeman.'

Student #2: 'Fireman.'

Student #3: 'Sex machine ...'

Overheard by m0ngch1ld, primary school
Posted on Tuesday, 16 October 2007

Southside liberalists

Was sitting in the Elephant & Castle restaurant with a few friends recently and there was a loud group of attractive southside girls (early 20s) seated beside us. Listening to them discuss the merits of new mothers breastfeeding in public, we hear one of them exclaim loudly, 'Well they're just FOCKING exhibitionists if you ask me!'

Overheard by Aoife, Temple Bar
Posted on Tuesday, 16 October 2007

Brotherly love

On the no. 10 bus, two brothers about seven years old:

Brother 1: 'Gimme one!' (sweets)

Brother 2: 'No!'

Brother 1: 'Gimme one or I'll fart on your face when you're asleep.'

Brother 2 hands pack of sweets to Brother 1!

Overheard by Dee, no. 10 bus
Posted on Monday, 15 October 2007

There's something about Mary

When Mary McAleese walked out onto the pitch to meet the players at Croke Park at the Ireland v Germany, one bloke shouted from the back of the Canal End, 'Go on, Mary, ye ride!'

Overheard by colin, Croker
Posted on Monday, 15 October 2007

FAI stuck in a time warp?

I was at the Ireland v Germany match at Croke Park. The Germans were making a substitution.

FAI announcer: 'Substitution for WEST Germany (ironic laughs from the crowd) ... eh, sorry, for Germany ...'

Overheard by G, Croke Park
Posted on Sunday, 14 October 2007

National stereotypes!

While driving four lads from Crumlin village to the Ireland v Germany game at Croke Park, the conversation got around to how sullen and devoid of humour the Germans are.

Guy in back of car: 'Bleeding Germans, no poxy fun, a grumpy shower altogether.' To which front-seat passenger pipes up these words of wisdom delivered without a trace of irony:

'You're dead right, Anto. Look at that Hitler fella, a right touchy bastard.'

I nearly wrote off the car trying to keep in the laughter.

Overheard by Damian, in my taxi on the way to Croke Park
Posted on Sunday, 14 October 2007

Post it note

I was in the queue in a post office and there was an aul' wan ahead of me. She says to the post mistress, 'Give us the stamps so I can post this parcel.'

The post mistress weighed the parcel and gave the aul' wan the parcel and the stamps. The aul' wan looked at the post mistress and asked, 'Will I stick 'em on meself?'

The post mistress says, without any hesitation, 'No love, stick them on the parcel!'

I nearly folded!

Overheard by Bello, post office in Clanbrassil Street
Posted on Sunday, 14 October 2007

At least he asked

A mate of mine was on the Nitelink a couple of years back, heading to Clonsilla. The bus was packed upstairs as it was 3 a.m.

A man up towards the top of the bus stands up and asks,

'Does anyone mind if I take a piss?'

At that, everyone lifts up their feet towards their chests, nothing said ...

Overheard by spilly, Nitelink to Clonsilla
Posted on Saturday, 13 October 2007

She'll give you a lift ...

Was visiting a friend in the IFSC. Stepped onto a lift with a few well-dressed financial types and, right at the back, there's two blokes in overalls covered in paint.

Female voice from lift: 'Please select floor.'

Bloke 1: 'Howya luv, that's a sexy voice ...'

Female voice from lift: 'Going down ...'

Bloke 2: 'Feckin' tease ... rawwrrrr ...'

Overheard by Fred, IFSC
Posted on Friday, 12 October 2007

Red-head

Eight-year-old Dub kid cycles by a guy with red hair and shouts, 'Here, Mister — do you read?'

Red-head says, 'Eh, yeah.'

Boy shouts, 'Have ye red pubes?'

Brilliant — even the red-head had to laugh!

Overheard by Anonymous, said to red-headed friend of mine
Posted on Friday, 12 October 2007

Decapitated?

Walking through Temple Bar, a group of young lads talking to a bouncer.

Lad: 'Here, mate, do you know where the Turk's Head is?'

Bouncer: 'I'd say it's probably on his shoulders!'

Overheard by Jean-Pierre, Temple Bar
Posted on Thursday, 11 October 2007

Two onions in a hanky

I was back home in Dublin on holidays recently, visiting my family. I was in Northside shopping centre with my mother. She was talking to a friend of hers whose husband had just died.

My Mother: 'That's terrible, I am very sorry to hear that.'

The woman replied: 'That old bastard, I am glad he's dead ... I needed two onions in a hanky so I could cry at the funeral!'

Overheard by Anonymous, Northside shopping centre
Posted on Thursday, 11 October 2007

No fingers all thumb

A mate of mine lost the four fingers of his right hand in an accident at work. After a couple of days we went to visit him in hospital and my brother asked if he would still be able to drive.

'Don't know, but I'd imagine so,' he answered.

My brother kept looking at him real serious and said,

'Sure, if you can't, you can hitch-hike everywhere!'

Overheard by Paul, hospital
Posted on Thursday, 11 October 2007

All on tap

My friend's sister came over to visit with her new baby. My friend's kids aged three and four were delighted with their new cousin. After a while the baby began to cry and the mother started to breastfeed.

The kids looked at each other in amazement. Not used to the spectacle, the four year old asked, 'What are ya doing?' and he was told, 'Feedin' da baby,' to which he replied,

'Do yis do Coke?'

Overheard by Bello, from my friend in Whitehall

Posted on Thursday, 11 October 2007

Finglas slang?

Some terms needed to understand: Locked = Drunk;

Boot = Ugly Girl

A girl and three lads were getting out of the car. The driver shouted to his friends, 'Is the boot locked?' and his friend answered, 'No, she's only had a couple of pints!'

Overheard by zazo5000, Finglas

Posted on Thursday, 11 October 2007

On the Nitelink

Stumbled onto the Nitelink home last Saturday night only to be caught in the crossfire between a group of skangers slagging each other off, from one side of the bus to the other.

The mouthy bird shouts to some fella, 'You were bleedin' shoii in bed anyway, so shut yer gob.'

To which he replies,

'Ah would ya ever f**k off, sure I only rode ya in me car.'

Overheard by Martha Focker, no. 42N bus
Posted on Thursday, 11 October 2007

Knickerbocker glory

I finished up work and went out shopping with my Mam. There was a girl that we kept seeing around the shop, and people kept assuming mistakenly that she worked there. While she was in the queue the security guard tapped her on the shoulder.

She, assuming someone was about to ask again, shouted at the top of her voice, 'I DON'T BLEEDIN' WORKKK HEERRRREEE WILLL YEEE EVERRRR CHANGEEE THE STUPIEH UNIFORMMMSSS.'

The security guard obviously didn't take to her shouting, and shouted back at the top of his voice,

'I KNOW YOU DON'T WORK HERE, I'M TELLING YOU YOUR SKIRT IS TUCKED INTO YOUR KNICKERS!'

The whole shop start laughing — funniest shopping trip ever!

Overheard by Carrie, Dunnes, The Square,
Tallaght, during Christmas rush
Posted on Thursday, 11 October 2007

Lovable skangers

Walking up O'Connell Street and two skanger young lads about 12 years old were chasing and beating the crap outta each other, calling each other every profanity under the sun.

Anyway, they gallop past me for the third time when one of them comes to a sudden halt beside a queue of people at a bus stop, where he spots a lady with twins in a buggy.

He shouts after Tommo, 'Tommo, Tommo, com 'ere, look at dis!'

Tommo gallops back to see what'z going on. When he sees the twins, the two skangers look at each other in amazement, all excited, and stick their heads in the buggy and start oooohing and aaaing!

Tommo: 'Ah, jaysis, they're luuuvly aren't they?'

'Yeah,' says the other lad, 'they're gaargeous, Missus, luuuvly.'

But they soon snapped out of it — and proceeded to kick the shite outta each other and gallop off again!

Overheard by Dee, O'Connell Street
Posted on Wednesday, 10 October 2007

Ah, how sweat!

A friend of mine is a primary school teacher in Dublin, teaching senior infants.

One wee boy in her class is from Russia. He has fairly good English but sometimes gets a bit mixed up. One day when they were doing computers he put up his hands and shouts, 'Teacher, teacher there's no rat with this computer.'

Overheard by Anonymous, friend teaching at a
Dublin primary school
Posted on Wednesday, 10 October 2007

The passion of the Religion teacher

Sitting in Religion in an all-girls school while a very awkward male teacher tries to explain the Catholic Church's views on sex. One of our other classmates, who was supposed to be playing a GAA match, comes in and starts explaining that the other team didn't show up.

This moved into a lengthy discussion about the 'cheek' of other school, when suddenly the Religion teacher, quite peeved at being forgotten shouts,

'CAN WE PLEASE TALK ABOUT SEX NOW!'

Overheard by Darrire, Sancta Maria College
Posted on Tuesday, 9 October 2007

Hygienic!

In changing rooms in Penney's, O'Connell Street, I overheard a young wan say to another, 'Dya know whaa, I've had a shower every single day this week!'

Overheard by dee, Penney's changing rooms
Posted on Tuesday, 9 October 2007

Magic water

Was in a newsagents a few weeks ago when a customer with a bottle of water approached the man behind the till.

Cashier: 'Next, please!'

Customer (showing the bottle of water): 'Is this Still water?'

Cashier (without hesitation): 'As far as I know it hasn't changed, yeh.'

Legend!

Overheard by Howie, Tallaght newsagents
Posted on Tuesday, 9 October 2007

À la carte Catholics

My seven-year-old son is preparing for his Holy Communion. We don't go to mass, so he was a bit in awe of the goings-on. It was a folk mass so there were plenty of alleluias ringing out from the altar.

My son nudged me, pointing at the singers, and whispered (loudly),

'Mom, are they the Christians?'

One mortified mom!

Overheard by Anonymous, church in Greystones
Posted on Monday, 8 October 2007

Big shoes to fill

A friend of mine had — by the age of 15 — reached the height of a healthy 6 foot 4 inches, with a size 14 foot to boot.

Shopping in town one day he had picked out a pair of runners to buy. A young fella came up to him after a while and asked, 'Can I help you there, bud?'

My mate asks, 'Do you have these in a size 14?'

The young lad looks at him in disbelief and
replies, 'Hold on till I see if we have a pair of
canoes out the back!'

Overheard by Cormac, town
Posted on Monday, 8 October 2007

Kids these days

I was driving through one of the estates in
Shankill.

There was a group of children playing on the
road just ahead of me so I slowed down as I was
passing them. When I looked out the window,
one of the kids who could have been no older
than five screams at me, 'Are ye startin!!'

Overheard by Susan, Shankill
Posted on Monday, 8 October 2007

Dub takes the biscuit

Amid a very stressful time for all my family in
Tallaght Hospital, my very sick mother
(thankfully well again) asked me to go to the
hospital shop and get her some plain biscuits.
Delighted that she wanted something to eat, I
eagerly obliged.

In the lift going back to the ward, biscuits in
hand, I met a middle-aged woman who asked,
'Are you on shop duty, love?' I replied that yes, I
was. What she said next gave us all a much
needed side-splitting laugh:

'Jaysus, love, the last time I done shop duty in
here, I was getting biscuits for me sick aunt, but
when I got back to her ward she was bleeding

dead.' Then touching my arm she looked at my plain biscuits and continued, 'You'll be alright though, luv — I bought the chocolate ones!'

Overheard by Deirdre, Tallaght Hospital
Posted on Sunday, 7 October 2007

Horsing around!

One night in the Sheriff youth club, two of the boys off the football team are undecided on a night on the town. One says to the other, 'John, are you goin' out?' which was met with the reply, 'Does a rockin' horse have a wooden dick!'

Overheard by G, Sheriff youth club
Posted on Saturday, 6 October 2007

The aliens have landed

While purchasing some stock for the club in a Cash & Carry, the following announcement came over the PA:

'Will the rep from Mars please report to reception.'

Overheard by jj, Cash & Carry Store
Posted on Friday, 5 October 2007

Lethal weapon

Two security guards on Henry Street last night over the walkie talkie:

'Lad in green combat trousers coming towards ye.'

'Yeah, what about him?'

'Is that the little bollix that hit me with the cauliflower?'

Overheard by Sheriff2, Henry Street
Posted on Friday, 5 October 2007

To kill a mocking bird

While waiting for the no. 123 bus at a stop in Summerhill, I noticed a man very obviously disoriented and out of his head (drugs/booze who knows) slumped against the wall.

Two minutes later a bird perched above him and shit on his head. It looked like someone threw a McFlurry at him, yet he didn't notice for maybe a minute or so, but when he noticed he threw an absolute fit.

He started to scream obscenities at the bird, mostly incoherent, but I did catch this classic line:

'See you, come here till I tell ya, come down here and I'll shit on your face!'

The bird declined!

Overheard by cactus, Summerhill
Posted on Wednesday, 3 October 2007

Perfect strangers

An elderly Dublin lady is taking a stroll around the Irish Museum of Modern Art with a friend when she passes someone she seems to recognise on the stairs. Typically Irish, she knows it would be rude not to acknowledge this person who seems so familiar.

'Ah, howyeh!' she places a gentle hand on the stranger's arm.

'Eh, hello,' the familiar gentleman replies.

'How's it goin'? Haven't been talkin' to ya in a while.'

'Erm, no ... eh ... I'm good.'

'Ah, dat's great, yer lookin' well.'

'Eh, thanks.'

'And how's yer Ma keepin?'

'Oh ... eh ... fine, she's fine ... I have to be on my way. Bye now.'

The familiar gentleman continues on his way. Once out of earshot the old lady's friend exclaims, 'Jaysus, Mary!'

'Whah?' replies Mary

'That was Elton John!'

Overheard by Anonymous, Irish Museum of Modern Art
Posted on Wednesday, 3 October 2007

Are you there Michael??

Was in one of these 'Angel' shops the other day — you know these places that sell mystical/spiritual items such as CDs, angel cards, and also perform healing. A customer was telling a story to other customers about when she went to visit a medium to try and contact her dead husband. The shopkeeper was listening in the background. It was a very sensitive subject. She was at the part when the medium got in touch with some spirits:

Customer: 'Then the medium said that on one side she has come in contact with a person, but is not sure of his name, and on the other side she has a Mickey' (the customer's dead husband's name!).

Shop Keeper: 'Is that his only body part she had?'

Overheard by Anonymous, in an Angel shop/healers
Posted on Wednesday, 3 October 2007

Extra body parts

A little boy snuggled onto his rather well-endowed auntie's lap. While staring at her cleavage he shouts, 'Ma, Auntie Phil has a bum on her belly.'

Overheard by Greystones, Harbour Bar in Bray
Posted on Wednesday, 3 October 2007

Service with attitude

I work as cabin crew for a budget airline and one day after take-off from Dublin Airport I was serving a rather posh woman. She asked me for an OJ.

I was well aware this meant orange juice, however she obviously felt the need to explain it, quoting, 'That's an orange juice to you dear!'

Feeling quite offended by this, I decided if you can't beat them join them, and promptly replied, 'Would you like ice, Mam? That's frozen water to you!'

Overheard by trollydollyx, on a flight from Dublin to London Gatwick
Posted on Wednesday, 3 October 2007

If you have to ask ...

Overheard in a pub off Grafton Street last week, early afternoon drink. A lady from one of the Brown Thomas make-up counters walks in, all dolled up in red uniform, full face on, looking like Mrs Bouquet. Hubbie in suit, looking beleaguered, carrying all her parcels (M&S bags, loads of them). She moves seat two or three times before finding one hygienic enough to please.

She orders a seafood something for both of them and decides to match it with a suitable wine.

Her quarter bottle arrives. 'Em, excuse me, barman,' (looking at bottle with a sigh) 'can you tell me where this "wine" has come from?'

Barman: 'The fridge ...'

She just sat down. Sniggers all round.

Overheard by Anonymous, Neary's cocktail lounge
Posted on Wednesday, 3 October 2007

The menu

Working in a restaurant in Malahide, standing talking with a colleague while waiting for a particular table to get seated. As they proceeded to check out the menu, one AJH (ah jaysus howya) turns to the other and asked,

'Ma, wha ya havin' for starters?'

The reply was, 'I was goin' to have the prawn cocktail, but I don't like the texture in me mouth, 'n anyways they don't taste the same as a package a' Skips!'

Overheard by Alan, at work
Posted on Tuesday, 2 October 2007

The Guinness gobshites

Working in a pub on the northside, two lads stand outside smoking when the Guinness delivery arrives. After taking off the large kegs, they roll a few half-size kegs past the lads.

One turns to the other and says, 'I wonder what's in them?' Without a moment's hesitation the other guy says,

'They're the glasses of Guinness, ya gobshite!'

Overheard by Nick, northside pub
Posted on Monday, 1 October 2007

Sensitive parenting

Was on the train from Dublin to Carlow. A group of women in their thirties sat near me and started discussing the bullying that was going on in their kids' school. One woman struck me as a really good mother, telling her son to tell teachers, and making him feel good.

After a few minutes, she mentioned she had run

into the kid that was bullying her son and told him,

'If you ever come near my Johnny again, I'll kill your parents with a baseball bat and bury them in the Dublin mountains and you'll never see them again.'

I nearly fell off my seat and spent the rest of the journey buried in my book!

Overheard by Eimer, on the train
Posted on Monday, 1 October 2007

Planet Ireland

In Maths class recently:

Teacher: 'Michael, what planet are you living on?'

Michael: 'Ireland ...'

Overheard by Anonymous, Maths class
Posted on Monday, 1 October 2007

Latest invention

Dublin woman in Jonesboro Market at a garden ornament stall.

Woman: 'What's that?'

Salesman: 'That's a sun dial.'

Woman: 'What does it do?'

Salesman: 'When the sun shines on it you can tell the time.'

Woman: 'What will they think of next ...'

Overheard by Pat, Jonesboro Market
Posted on Sunday, 30 September 2007

The art of movement

On the no. 18 bus on the Long Mile Road. The bus was packed and the driver wouldn't move until people moved back. There was a really tall man in the aisle and he was told to move or else the bus wouldn't move. Frustrated, a woman shouted at him:

'Move back! It's like movin' forwards except backwards!'

Overheard by J, no. 18 bus
Posted on Sunday, 30 September 2007

Read it

While getting my post from a busy apartment lobby the other morning a resident came in and spoke to a guy by the ESB meters:

Resident: 'You're right to check your meter — that crowd did me by €60 on my last bill.'

Guy: 'I am that crowd ... I'm the meter reader!'

Overheard by Sarah, apartment lobby
Posted on Friday, 28 September 2007

Brendan Neeson?

Last year my Mam was in my next-door neighbour's house and the *Late Late* was on. Brendan Gleeson was being interviewed and after a few minutes of watching, this conversation unfolded between the ladies:

Mam: 'Barry Gleeson is on the telly!'

Neighbour: 'God, he's the image of his brother.'

Mam: 'Who's his brother?'

Neighbour: 'Brendan Gleeson?'

Mam: 'Oh, sorry, no, that is Brendan Gleeson! I just got the name wrong!'

Neighbour: 'Oh, right. And isn't he a brother of Liam Neeson?'

Mam: (silent disbelief)

Neighbour: 'They're gettin' the picture of each other, though I'd say Liam is older.'

Overheard by Anonymous, at home
Posted on Thursday, 27 September 2007

The land of no return

On the DART home from work I overheard two elderly ladies having a chat.

Lady #1: 'It's awful, when I was coming in this morning a man collapsed on the carriage. I think he had a heart-attack. I must watch the news tonight. If he died they might give it a mention.'

Lady #2: 'Oh God, that's horrible. I hope he didn't buy a return ticket!'

Overheard by The Ballhopper, the DART
Posted on Thursday, 27 September 2007

Bertie, your people are starving

Overseen rather than Overheard

Man protesting outside the Dáil with a notice board that reads:

'On hunger strike until Bertie comes clean and tells the truth to the Mahon Tribunal.'

He was drinking a cup of coffee — with a Twix!

Overheard by Gaz, outside the Dáil
Posted on Thursday, 27 September 2007

Traffic cops

While driving on the M50 recently with my sister, brother-in-law and 12-year-old nephew, we were overtaken by a Garda Traffic Corps jeep with 'Garda Traffic Corps' in big letters down the side.

My nephew turned to me in all seriousness and asked, 'Why is there an 'R' in traffic cops?'

Overheard by Shane, M50
Posted on Thursday, 27 September 2007

Request

In the local the other day there were two lads playing guitars. After they finished a song someone shouted to them, 'Here, do yes do requests?'

They said they did.

'Well f*ck off, cause you're bleeding brutal!'

Overheard by sheriff2, Clonliffe House
Posted on Wednesday, 26 September 2007

Age is relative

Shortly after my aunt gave birth to her son, her brother Dan was speaking to their other brother Mike (who lives in the States) on the phone.

Uncle Mike: 'So, I hear Kate had a young fella.'

Uncle Dan: 'Yeah. He was fairly young alright.'

Overheard by Ether, via my Mam
Posted on Tuesday, 25 September 2007

The generation gap exposed

I was at the local supermarket when I passed a boy and his mother, he with a pack of CDs in hands and his mother angrily telling him, 'I'm not payin' a tenner for you to burn CDs, what ya wanna do that fer anyway, is it stupid ya think I am or wa?'

Overheard by Anonymous, Dunnes, ILAC Centre
Posted on Tuesday, 25 September 2007

It's in the jeans

Was sitting outside a pub in town, a couple of lads at the table beside us. A girl walks by in a

pair of Rock & Republic jeans. One of the guys at the table beside us shouts out, '€600 for a pair of jeans and your arse still looks shite!'

Overheard by keepitrim, Dublin 2
Posted on Tuesday, 25 September 2007

Like a needle in a haystack ...

I regularly have a coffee in a coffee-shop on D'Olier Street and it takes me past this nice, softly-spoken bloke from Dublin Bus. I think he must be a supervisor or something.

One day, I overheard him talking calmly into his walkie-talkie: 'And tell us, by any chance, did you ever find that bus?'

Overheard by Anonymous, D'Olier Street
Posted on Tuesday, 25 September 2007

Organ-asms!

Was in Biology class and the topic was 'organisms'.

My friend, quite ditsy but genuine, was asked a question by the teacher in front of about 50 others (lecture style):

Teacher: 'Jessica what are organisms?'

Jessica: 'Orgasms are ... '(class erupts in laughter and what was funnier was the fact that she didn't realise what everyone's laughin' at)

Teacher: 'Or-gan-isms, Jessica ...!'

Jessica: 'Oh sorry, Miss, yea, ehm, organ-asms are ...' (another eruption)

Teacher: 'ORGAN-ISMS, JESSICA, ORGAN-ISMS!'

Jessica (in a fluster): 'I KNOW, MISS, I KNOW, I JUST CAN'T SAY IT, I JUST CAN'T SAY IT, I TRY BUT ORGASMS KEEPS CUMIN' OUT!'

Overheard by Chloe, sixth-year Biology class
Posted on Tuesday, 25 September 2007

Misheard Lyrics

I was collecting my younger sister and her friends from swimming lessons a couple of years back. The song 'Brimful of Asha' was on the radio and we were all singing happily along. All of a sudden everyone went quiet and one of my sister's friends was heard singing at the top of her lungs, serious as anything,

'There was a binful of rashers on the 45!'

Overheard by K.C., my car
Posted on Monday, 24 September 2007

Utilities!

Overheard a woman saying she had no room in her kitchen and, 'Would love to get one of those fertility rooms built on the side of her house for her washing machine and all the other big appliances.'

Overheard by Catherine, Submarine Bar
Posted on Monday, 24 September 2007

Never judge a book by its cover!

Nice, polite family gathering. The topic gets around to Superman. The kids are in full flight, describing him to elderly Auntie. They get to the bit where they tell her, '... but as soon as he takes all his clothes off, he's Superman!'

Auntie leaves us all breathless with her instant response:

'Aren't we all!'

Overheard by Anonymous, at home,
Montpelier Gardens, Dublin 7
Posted on Monday, 24 September 2007

Left-hand Granny

Out with my grandparents a few years ago, I spotted a foreign registered car driving along. I said to my grandfather, 'Look, Granda, a car with left-hand drive.' My grandmother then says, 'God, that's great, they have everything for left-handers these days!'

Overheard by Alan, driving in Dublin
Posted on Sunday, 23 September 2007

MTV

In my local, Egans in Kilkenny, a couple of Dubs walk in, big hoop earrings, peroxide heads — you know the type. One of them spots the TV:

'Jayus, look they have MTV down here too!'

'We only have a lend of it, we have to give it back to the pub next door in an hour,' replied the barman.

'What a pity,' they say — and walk out!

Overheard by murty, Egans, John Street, Kilkenny
Posted on Sunday, 23 September 2007

A rubbish name for the Ha'penny Bridge!

Waiting to cross the road at the Ha'penny Bridge, I heard an American tourist ask another, 'What's the name of this bridge?' He spotted a word on a bin at the corner and said, 'It's the Bruscar Bridge!'

Overheard by Brenda, at the Ha'penny Bridge
Posted on Sunday, 23 September 2007

Wee Daniel

I was upstairs on the tourist bus going around Dublin. There were some English tourists from Liverpool who were quite loud.

As we drove down O'Connell Street and passed by the statue of Daniel O'Connell, the driver said, 'On our right is a statue of an important Irish figure, Daniel O'Connell.'

On hearing this, one of the English women was shocked and exclaimed in a loud voice,

'I can't believe that the Irish built a statue to that bloody singer!'

Overheard by Jacko, Dublin tourist bus
Posted on Saturday, 22 September 2007

First aid cop

Man collapses in St Stephen's Green and a large crowd gathers around him. A garda goes to his aid and is trying to help him breathe.

Suddenly a man pushes his way to the front of

the crowd and asks the cop, 'Do you need help?'

The garda asks, 'Are you a doctor?'

The man says, 'No, I'm a dentist.'

Garda replies, 'Well, when he has a toothache —
we'll call you!'

Overheard by Bob, St Stephen's Green

Posted on Saturday, 22 September 2007

Institute Geography classes urgently needed!

In the Institute last week, overheard these two
D4 girls on the corridor:

Girl 1: 'Sorry, loike, I didn't catch your name?
I'm Aimee with loike, two Es? And yours?'

Girl 2: 'It's, loike, Maria with one R.'

After a couple of 'haw haw haw haw haws', Girl
1 asks, 'I'm from Sandymount, and you?'

Girl 2: 'Oh, I'm from Cavan, big estate.'

(long awkward pause)

Girl 1: 'So is that, loike, the southside or the
northside?'

Girl 2: (just gives her daggers)

Girl 1: 'What, is it in Wicklow?'

Overheard by Anonymous, Institute of Education, Leeson Street

Posted on Saturday, 22 September 2007

In a time zone all of her own

Watching the France v Ireland rugby match in my
house with a group of friends. One of our

friends, Colm, was over in France at the time.

Richie: 'Here lads, Colm's in France and they're an hour ahead of us. Will I ring him and see what the score is?' (he was of course joking)

Charlene: 'NO! NO! NO! I don't want to know what the score is before seeing the match!'

Ha-ha — we all had a good laugh at that!

Overheard by Andrea, Dún Laoghaire
Posted on Friday, 21 September 2007

The advantage of having a wheelchair

I was standing outside a busy bar on Baggot Street with a few friends when a gent approaches in a wheelchair. He took a look towards the door, looked towards us and said, 'It looks way too busy to go in there.'

At this point my mate piped up, 'I don't know what your problem is, sure you already have a seat.'

Thankfully, the chap in the wheelchair took it well and saw the funny side!

Overheard by The Ballhopper, Toners, Baggot Street
Posted on Friday, 21 September 2007

Drunk and disorderly

Was at an ATM machine one night in Ranelagh and was hassled for change by a homeless guy. At first I was trying to ignore him but couldn't avoid overhearing his rant about how he had earlier been picked up for being drunk and disorderly.

In the thickest Dublin accent you can imagine, this is what he said:

'How the hell can ya be drunk and disorderly when you're asleep?'

Overheard by David, AIB Ranelagh
Posted on Thursday, 20 September 2007

The specialist

A true Dub, sitting at the bar, talking on his phone:

'I'm no gynaecologist, but I'll have a look!'

Overheard by James, Anseo, Camden Street
Posted on Thursday, 20 September 2007

Can I help you? Obviously not!

At Dublin Airport baggage hall a lady walked up to an airport staff member when her bags failed to appear after she arrived.

Lady: 'My bags haven't come out yet.'

Staff Member: 'Has your plane landed yet?'

Overheard by Santos L Helper, in Dublin Airport
Posted on Wednesday, 19 September 2007

Tongue tied

At work in a CD manufacturer we needed a few discs to be tested but they were in a different department. My workmate gets on the phone:

'Hi, who's that? ...

Heya, Margaret, would you be able to pull a

couple of dicks for me? Eh, COUPLE OF DISCS, sorry — a couple of discs?'

Overheard by Tucker, in work
Posted on Wednesday, 19 September 2007

Go on there, get that into your lungs!

Two auld fellas of about 60+ sitting on a park bench, enjoying a rare day of sunshine after a miserable summer.

'Jaysus, isn't life grand all the same?'

'It is too, y'know, sometimes all I need is some fresh air and a cigarette!'

Overheard by Fenster, Fairview Park
Posted on Tuesday, 18 September 2007

Classy bird

After a gig in Vicar Street, queues a mile long for the toilets. One of the lads says to his girlfriend, 'F**k this, I'm going outside.'

His girlfriend says, 'I'm not pissing on the street tonight — I'm in my nice dress!'

Overheard by berta, Vicar Street
Posted on Tuesday, 18 September 2007

Lisp and a northern accent, not a good combination

Guy comes into a builders providers on the Naas Road, with a very strong Northern Irish accent plus a bad lisp.

The man asks for 'shifter bits'.

Guy behind counter: 'Shifter bits?'

Lispy: 'Yeah, shifter bits.'

Counter Guy: 'What's a shifter bit?'

Lispy: 'Bits, bits ...'

Counter Guy: 'Like a drill bit or an adjustable spanner?'

Lispy: 'NO! NO! NO!' (getting pissed off) 'Jeshsus, shifter bits size 8.'

Counter Guy (looking confused): 'Eh, maybe it's a special tool you'd get in a motor factors?'

Lispy: 'Ah, for jeshsus shake!' (man points at a display behind counter) 'Them shifter bits there, are ya shtupid or shomething?'

Counter Guy (turns to the display): 'Aaw, safety boots size 8, no worries!' (while biting his lip!)

Overheard by Anonymous, Heiton's builders providers, Naas Road

Posted on Monday, 17 September 2007

Technugly

Overheard in Ibiza by a group of Dubs beside the pool:

Lad 1: 'Look at yer one!'

Lad 2: 'Would ya stop, big Eircom broadband head on her.'

Lad 1: 'What?'

Lad 2: 'In a bundle!'

Overheard by Stephen, Bariva Apartments, Ibiza

Posted on Saturday, 15 September 2007

A what?

I was next in line with my son to see Santa one Christmas. In front of me was a guy and a little girl and he was asking her what do you say when Santa asks you what you want from him. She says a doll, a bike and something else. It was all very cute. Anyway when she eventually got to see Santa I could overhear the following:

Santa: 'So, little girl, have you been good girl?'

Little Girl: 'Yes.'

Santa: 'So, what do you want from Santa?'

Little Girl: 'A six foot cow!'

Overheard by Anonymous, Santa's grotto
Posted on Friday, 14 September 2007

Overheard on Ballymun bus

Many years ago, I stayed in digs in Glasnevin whilst attending Bolton Street College. One morning I was upstairs on the early morning Ballymun bus into the city. The bus was jammed and a kid whose mother was at the back was running up and down the aisle with a dirty big lollipop! Everyone was pushing in as the kid passed, in case their coats got ruined by the sticky lollipop.

The mother, seeing what was happening, was screaming to the kid, 'Michael, come down here now and sit down next to me.'

After a few minutes of this, the kid turned from the front of the bus and shouted back, 'Mammy, you leave me alone or I'll tell all the people on the bus that you did your wee wee in my potty this morning.'

Overheard by John, Ballymun bus into city
Posted on Friday, 14 September 2007

Can you please abbreviate?

Friend: 'Got your mail and by the way, what does BTW mean?'

Overheard by Anonymous, from a friend
Posted on Friday, 14 September 2007

Not the brightest

Walking along the Grand Canal on a typical rainy day. My friend Jo says, 'Aw, look at the poor swans hiding under the water ... they don't want to get wet!'

Overheard by Anonymous, Harolds Cross
Posted on Tuesday, 11 September 2007

Those were the days

Really old man, hardly walking, heading down O'Connell Street, hanging off of the arm of (who seemed to be) his daughter.

'Jaynee, how things change,' says he.

She seemed to be half ignoring the poor chap.

'I remember the Nelsons Pillar, Angela. If you met a young wan there it was said that — with a little bit of luck — you'd get your nuts.'

She looked mortified!

Overheard by Anonymous, O'Connell Street
Posted on Monday, 10 September 2007

Viva Las Skerries!

Was having a few beers with friends in a mate's house and got a game of cards going. While we were getting the cards ready a friend volunteered to go to the shop to get supplies. We asked him to get a box of matches so we could use them as chips for poker.

He returned, saying that the shop had no matches — but he'd got a lighter instead!

Overheard by P, mate's house
Posted on Monday, 10 September 2007

Hard of hearing?

Walking over Portobello Bridge one morning, running late.

Pissing rain. Freezing cold. Traffic mad. Everyone miserable. You get the picture.

The path on the bridge was crowded so it was slow.

Thirty-something woman beside me says to a little auld one in passing, maybe in her seventies:

'Ah, howaya Miriam. How ye keepin, haven't seen ye in bleedin' aaages? Jayzuz, isn't eh' a'ter getting' real cold?'

To which your one goes,

'Ah, would you ever f**k off, you're not lookin' too young there yourself!'

Overheard by LongMileRoad, Portobello
Posted on Sunday, 9 September 2007

Charmer

A group of girls were sitting in the smoking room at the local pub. They were asking people who came in, 'How old do you think I am?' and so forth.

When one of the regulars came into the smoking room, he was asked, 'Here, how old do I look?'

He replied, 'I don't know, but if you sit on my face, I'll guess your weight!'

Overheard by JUNIORF, in the smoking room at the local
Posted on Thursday, 6 September 2007

Wake-up call

I was on my way to work in Dublin early one cold winter's morning a few years back, and said 'Good morning' to an elderly man as I passed him.

'Listen, love,' he replied, 'any morning I can throw me bollix out of the bed and follow them is a good morning!'

Overheard by Anonymous, Omni car park
Posted on Thursday, 6 September 2007

Kids really do say the funniest things

I'd just got home from work to find the eight year old jumping up and down with excitement at an upcoming party. She was bursting with questions: 'What will I wear? What can I bring?'

With a thousand other immediate things to do right away, I told her to wait till later — this party was the last thing on my mind.

About 10 minutes later she sidled up to me again with the question, 'Maaaaammm! Are you at the end of your mind yet?'

Overheard by Anonymous, at home, Dublin 7
Posted on Thursday, 6 September 2007

Foot in mouth!

A DIY-er in a major hardware outlet, discussing the size of an extractor fan he wanted for his kitchen.

DIY-er: '... not sure about the size ...'

Assistant: 'Well then, wouldn't you like to go home and measure your hole?'

Overheard by Anonymous, B & Q
Posted on Wednesday, 5 September 2007

Bad choice of words?

Arrived in the village to post a letter, only to find a postman crouched on his hunkers emptying the letterbox. To my absolute horror I heard myself say, 'Do you mind if I give you one?'

Couldn't get away fast enough!

Overheard by Anonymous, a village somewhere in County Dublin
Posted on Tuesday, 4 September 2007

Foreigners?

At a bus stop in Ringsend, two true-blue Dubs having a conversation about their work colleagues. The boyos appeared to be builders of some sort, and one said to the other,

'Jaysus, dis lad I'm workin' wit, I can never understand a word he is saying.' The other responded, 'Why? Is he foreign?' to which the other replied, 'No, he's English!'

Overheard by Louis, Ringsend
Posted on Saturday, 1 September 2007

Nice compliment

During the Dublin and Kerry match last week, Diarmuid Murphy the Kerry keeper was getting a bit of stick from the Dubs on the Hill when someone shouted down,

'Diarmuid, you have a head like a melted welly!'

Overheard by Eoin, Hill 16
Posted on Thursday, 30 August 2007

Political confusion

At the recent match between Dublin and Derry, I had the pleasure of standing in front of an opinionated Dub fan, with an obvious abundance of political ideology. His first rant was directed clearly at the Garda Band at half time: 'FREE STATE BASTARDS'

He's clearly of a republican persuasion, I thought, but his republican credentials were somewhat tarnished when he began his second rant, directed at the Derry fans: 'BLEEDIN' ENGLISH BASTARDS, SHUDIN' EVEN BE PLAYING FOOTBALL IT'S A BLEEDIN' 32-COUNTY ALL-IRELAND GAME, NO BLEEDIN' ENGLISH GAME'

I — along with others — was in fits of laughter at this. I had to turn around and put a face to the stupidity, and yes, he was every inch I pictured him — right down to the silly moustache.

Overheard by Dave, Hill 16
Posted on Tuesday, 28 August 2007

Well at least he had the manners to inform me

I got onto the no. 78A bus, found no seats downstairs so decided to try upstairs. I found an empty seat and was about to sit down when some bloke yells,

'HERE, MISSUS, I wouldn't sit there if I were you, I just pissed there!'

Overheard by Roisin, no. 78A bus
Posted on Tuesday, 28 August 2007

Fallen comrades

Me: 'Hi, I'm hoping to get a taxi back to Glasnevin.'

Woman: 'Okay, where are you now?'

Me: 'Terenure College.'

Woman: 'Okay, where's that?'

Me: 'Em, Terenure.'

Woman (sighs then sarky): 'Thanks ...'

Me: 'No, sorry, I'm not being smart, I'm not from here. I just know it's Terenure College. I don't know the street names outside.'

Woman: 'Well can you not look at the signs?'

Me: 'Afraid not, the main gate is a good distance away from where I'm standing now.'

Woman: 'That wasn't very clever. How are we going to find you?'

Me: 'It's a school ... you can come up the drive. I'll be the only person standing around.'

Woman (laughs now): 'But WHERE in Terenure is the school?'

Me (laughing): 'You guys dropped me here this morning from Glasnevin. You lot stranded me out here in the first place, so SOMEONE there knows where it is.'

Woman (laughing): 'Fine ... be half an hour.'

When I get in the cab, the driver gets on the radio: 'Mary, have found Lost Northsider and am returning to base ...'

Mary: 'Roger that, Sean ... we never leave a man behind.'

Overheard by Fred, Terenure College
Posted on Sunday, 26 August 2007

Tiger Kidnapping

My 18-year-old brother was playing footie on a green in Swords with his mates, this was during the whole 'tiger kidnapping' scandals with the bank managers and stuff. Anyway, on this particular day one of the kidnappings occured in one of the houses on the green where he was playing so the police call him in for questioning as a possible witness.

Garda: 'Now, tell me what you saw, anything suspicious, anyone just hanging around that you didn't recognise?'

Bro: 'No, saw nothing really, mad though, I wuda thought I'd hav noticed "that" like!!'

Garda: 'What do you mean by "that"??'

Bro: 'Well deffo wuda noticed if I saw a tiger around Swords, didn't think people could have tigers as pets ... deffo not playing round there again, I'd be sh***in' meself if it escaped!!'

Overheard by Jenny, Swords
Posted on Friday, 25 August 2007

Location Location Location

I rang a restaurant during the week to book a table. I wasn't quite sure of the location so I asked, 'Where exactly are you?' The waiter replied,

'I'm standing in front of the till next to the door!'

Overheard by kopfile, Little Caesars
Posted on Friday, 24 August 2007

Very Lost

Outside a bus stop in Trinity College an American came up to me with a map and asked,

'Which road do I take to get to Belgium?'

Overheard by Tom, bus stop outside Trinity
Posted on Friday, 24 August 2007

Pizzas and buckets

Was in an Italian restaurant on Dame Street the other night. Two girls sit down at the table next to me and my girlfriend, and one of the girls ask for a pizza.

Girl #1: 'How big are your pizzas?'

Waiter: 'Nine inch, 12 inch ...'

Girl #1: 'How big is the 9 inch?'

Waiter laughing: 'About the size of the plate in front of you.'

Girl #1: 'And what's the difference between the 9 inch and the 12 inch?'

Waiter: 'Three inches!'

Girl #1: 'I don't know, I'll just order chicken wings.'

Girl #2: 'I'll have those as well and will ya give us one of those things that comes in a bucket with the ice as well?'

Waiter: 'A bucket?'

Girl #2: 'Ye know, the bottles.'

Waiter: 'You mean wine or champagne?'

Girl #2: 'Yeah one of those, the nicest ones.'

Waiter walks off ...

Girl #1: 'Bleeding Italians don't having a bleeding clue what they're talking about.'

Overheard by John, Dame Street
Posted on Friday, 24 August 2007

Clear as ...

Walking through the corridor in St Aidan's CBS, Whitehall, when I overheard a teacher called Mr McCrystal giving out to a young lad.

Mr McCrystal: 'Now I won't have that anymore, you got that, never again. Am I clear?'

Young Lad: 'Yes, sir, Mc-crystal clear.'

Overheard by Dunid, St Aidan's CBS, Whitehall
Posted on Friday, 24 August 2007

My Nan

My Nanny is chatting to her friends in the pub:

Nanny: 'My nephew is living in Australia for the

past 12 years, he's a paedophile.'

People didn't know what to say ...

Nanny: 'Ye, he drives an ambulance!'

Oh, *paramedic*!

Overheard by Sheriff2, pub
Posted on Friday, 24 August 2007

Metric spuds

Overheard in fruit & veg market:

Old Lady: 'Can I have five pounds of potatoes, please.'

Market Trader: 'Sorry luv, it's now kilos.'

Old Lady: 'Ok, can I have five pounds of kilos please!'

Overheard by RayG, fruit & veg market
Posted on Thursday, 23 August 2007

A worse alternative?

Sitting at home with me niece one morning and she asked for some popcorn. Me Ma turns around and says, 'No, no, love, it's too early for popcorn. Do you want some cake instead?'

Overheard by Nx, at home
Posted on Thursday, 23 August 2007

Culture differences

I was out having a smoke in the local when I overheard three heads having a heated discussion about the recent turban-wearing Sikh garda, and heard this classic:

'Sure, give them a few years and they'll be patrolling O'Connell Street on elephants!'

Overheard by phil, the local
Posted on Wednesday, 22 August 2007

Kids are mad!

Was talking to my friend the other night, with his three-year-old son who's a very cheeky chappy indeed!

I took out a packet of sweets and offered the kid one. After taking it, his father asks, 'Now son, what do you say if a stranger offers you sweets?' The kid replies 'Yes!'

Disgusted at his reply my mate says in a very firm tone, 'What! No, that's not what you say! What do you say if a stranger offers you bleedin' sweets?!'

Kid shoots back, 'Yes ... PLEASE!'

Overheard by Anonymous, mate's house
Posted on Wednesday, 22 August 2007

A caring Dub

One half of a mobile phone conversation, in Abbey Street yesterday:

'Ah, how's it going, John?'

PAUSE

'C'mere to me, were ye caught in the hurricane?'

PAUSE
'Ye big sap!'

Overheard by Dean, Abbey Street
Posted on Wednesday, 22 August 2007

Ty-ezz fer by-ezz

I went into a children's clothes shop in Tallaght and asked the shop assistant if they stocked ties, as my young son wanted one.

She said, looking at me as if I had several heads, 'Ty-ez? Yer lookin' for Tyy-ezz?'

'Yes', I answered, 'do you have any?'

'We don't have any roo-em for ty-ez.' She then added, 'There's the biggest tie shop in Ireland round the bleedin' corner, for f*** sake.'

It took me a moment to realise she was referring to Smyths, the TOY shop!

Overheard by Katie, Tallaght
Posted on Tuesday, 21 August 2007

Motherly instinct

Sitting in front of me on the Luas, a small lad about three or four years old is talking to his grandmother: 'Nan, my Ma says I'm never to talk to strangers.'

'Yes, your mother is right, love,' says Gran.

After a fairly long pause of about two minutes the kid says to Gran, 'Nan, what's a stranger?'

Overheard by Phil, Luas Jervis Street
Posted on Tuesday, 21 August 2007

Burglars

When one of my brothers was in primary school, it was the first day back after the summer and the teacher was asking the kids about their holidays. One girl shot her hand in the air, gasping to tell her most exciting news.

'Miss, our house was burgled!'

'Oh, that's terrible, Fiona, do they know who did it?'

'My Daddy said it was gobshites!'

Overheard by Kev, St Mary's primary school
Posted on Monday, 20 August 2007

In the Know

On the FM104 radio phone show there was a heated discussion about the case of the Sikh man who was refused entry into the Garda reserve force unless he stopped wearing his turban on duty.

This Dublin young fellah gets on and drawls, 'The garda were right, I mean if he arrested me I'd wanna see the top of his head so I know what's goin' on like, you know what I mean?'

The mind boggles ...

Overheard by Sara, FM104
Posted on Monday, 20 August 2007

Like father like son

A very long time ago when I was on a school outing we went to the National Gallery. One of the lads, Tom,* was the son of a notorious Dublin criminal, who was in hiding at the time. We had a guided tour and at the end we had some time to ask some questions. Tom got really excited and asked the tour guide a million questions.

'Which painting is worth the most?'

'Are there sensors on the walls?'

'How many security guards are on at night?' (you get the picture)

The tour guide was really impressed by his enthusiasm ...

*Name changed for obvious reasons.

Overheard by C, The National Gallery

Posted on Monday, 20 August 2007

Star struck

11 August, two young girls on the bus.

Girl 1: 'Do you want me to read you out your stars?'

Girl 2: 'No, I don't believe in them.'

Girl 1: 'What ... they are soooo true.'

Girl 2: 'Go on so.'

Girl 1: 'OK then, what's your sign?'

Girl 2: 'Virgo.'

Girl 1 (ruffles through the page looking for Virgo then in absolute amazement): 'I don't believe it!'

Girl 2: 'Oh my God, what is it, what's it say?'

Girl 1: 'A hectic time; with your birthday only around the corner, plans need to be made ...'

Girl 2 interrupting: 'It knows about me 18th?'

Girl 1: 'I told ya, it's always right.'

Overheard by Dunid, bus in Drumcondra
Posted on Monday, 20 August 2007

Big mouth Dad

I was waiting for the bus on Dame Street and was explaining to my Dad (who is English) how southsiders and northsiders generally tend to slag each other. Being from the southside, I told him how we say all the scumbags are from the northside (not true of course, there's plenty on the south!).

We get on the bus and sit down. Dad looks around and says in a really loud voice in his

posh English accent, 'This bus looks like it's full
of northsiders!'

All I could say was 'Shhhhhhhhhhhhh!' and just
glared at him, stared straight ahead and hoped
nobody heard a thing!

Overheard by Anonymous, on the bus
Posted on Friday, 17 August 2007

Elevated

An elderly woman steps from the DART at
Glenageary station and looks slightly unsure of
her bearings. A young Chinese man in an
Iarnród Éireann top is in the elevator, so the
elderly woman approaches him.

Elderly Woman: 'Is this Glenageary?'

Young Chinese Man (clearly with little
comprehension of English): 'What?'

Elderly Woman: 'Is this Glenageary station?'

Young Chinese Man (baffled): 'What?'

Elderly Woman (increasingly flustered): 'Is this
the DART stop for Glenageary?'

Young Chinese Man (triumphantly): 'No, this is
elevator!'

Doors shut, elevator goes up ...

Overheard by peter, Glenageary DART station
Posted on Wednesday, 15 August 2007

The dearest

While driving my taxi I had an elderly passenger
who said, 'You're the dearest taxi I have ever got

from this shopping centre, €6.47 and we haven't even left the shops!'

I looked at her and said, 'That's the time you're looking at — not the meter!'

Overheard by Anonymous, in my taxi
Posted on Tuesday, 14 August 2007

Mis-heard in Dublin

Was out in the pub last Friday with a few mates from work. One particular guy brought his brother in with him. His brother, who is gay, and himself recently bought an apartment together, something I'm also in the process of doing. So I saunter up to my mate's brother (who I shall call Dave) and the following exchange takes place:

Me: 'How's it going, Dave? Question for ya.'

Dave: 'Sure.'

Me: 'You're a home-owner now, right?'

Dave: 'What? I'm a homo?!'

Me: 'Home-owner! HOME-OWNER!'

Overheard by Pete, pub in the city centre
Posted on Tuesday, 14 August 2007

An audience with the commode

I spent some time in hospital at Christmas. The ward was full of elderly women. One woman was unable to walk so needed to use a commode (she called it the po). One morning she started screaming that she needed the po.

I rang the bell for the nurse, who was Filipino. She started explaining to her that it was very early — it was only 6.30 a.m. I thought that this was a bit cruel, so I called the nurse over and told her that the woman was looking for the commode.

The nurse put her head in her hands, started laughing, and told me she, 'thought the woman was saying she wanted to see the Pope!'

Overheard by Anonymous, Beaumont Hospital
Posted on Monday, 13 August 2007

When 1 + 1 doesn't ADD up

Talking to my sister about a relation of ours, I said, 'I think he has OCD.'

She says, 'No, he has ADD.'

I said, 'What's the difference?'

She said, 'OCD means you have to keep cleaning everything around you, and ADD means you're a little bollix!'

Overheard by Intel, at home having a few drinks
Posted on Monday, 13 August 2007

I guess this adds to the continuity

More overseen than overheard. On the train line between Connolly and Clontarf there's some graffiti saying 'CONTINUITUITY IRA'.

Some genius having trouble knowing when to *stop* spelling the name of the group they support is a new one on me ...

Overheard by Cian, the DART between Connolly and Clontarf
Posted on Friday, 10 August 2007

Mis-heard

Many years ago, repeating the Leaving Cert in Ringsend, I was taking in some quiet study time in the school library, in preparation for the exams. In walks the principal and utters what I thought was, 'Terrible stuffy in here.'

I replied, 'Yes, indeed,' and left it at that. Then once again the principal repeated what I thought was, 'Terrible stuffy in here.'

Again I replied, 'Yes, indeed.' I was asked by the principal to step outside and explain my cheek!

Getting to the bottom of it, she wanted to know if Terrence Duffy was here ... Confused or what?

Overheard by Emmet, Ringsend Dublin
Posted on Thursday, 9 August 2007

The 'M' word

In Biology class many years ago, studying the female reproductive system, the teacher asked what was the name for this monthly occurrence.

Johnny starts, 'Sir, sir,' really eager, which was unusual for this individual but obviously it was one of those rare times when he knew the answer and he wasn't going to miss out.

Teacher: 'Yes, Johnny?'

Johnny: 'Sir, sir, the masturbation cycle!'

We pissed ourselves ...

Overheard by seahorse, school
Posted on Thursday, 9 August 2007

Dublin schoolboy wit

Teacher at the end of Biology lesson:

'So, boys, what causes an erection?' (expecting the answer 'bloodflow to the penis, etc.')

Loooong embarrassed pause. Boy down the back of the class:

'YER MA!'

Overheard by Mrs Mogsey, local Bro's school
Posted on Wednesday, 8 August 2007

First date conversation

Was in a restaurant on Georges Street at the weekend and overheard the following conversation between a young couple sitting at the table next to me who looked as if they were on a first date.

Initially there is one of those long, awkward silences until the girl pipes up in her D4 accent, 'So, do you like jogging?'

There is another long silence until the guy, clearly confused by the question goes, 'Uh ... ya.'

To which she replies, 'Oh, I love jogging ... it's so much quicker than walking.'

Overheard by jonnyfu, restaurant on Georges Street
Posted on Tuesday, 7 August 2007

Don't argue with the gay flight attendant

My flight was being served by a camp flight attendant, who seemed to put everyone in a good mood as he served us food and drinks.

As the plane prepared to descend, he came swishing down the aisle and told us, 'Captain Marvey has asked me to announce that he'll be landing the plane shortly, so, lovely people, if you could just put your trays up, that would be super.'

On his trip back up the aisle, he noticed that an extremely well-dressed and exotic young woman hadn't moved a muscle.

'Perhaps you didn't hear me over those big brute engines, but I asked you to raise your tray, so the main man can pop us on the ground.'

She calmly turned her head and said, 'In my country, I am called a Princess and I take orders from no one.'

To which the flight attendant replied, without missing a beat, 'Well, sweet-cheeks, in my country I'm called a Queen, so I out-rank you. Tray up, Bitch.'

Overheard by beets, Delta flight to New York
Posted on Tuesday, 7 August 2007

Off to Funtasia

My brother's friend was over and was telling us he's going on holidays next week.

I asked where he'll be going and he said, 'Funtasia.'

He's actually going to Tunisia ...

Overheard by L, at home
Posted on Monday, 6 August 2007

Chips with everything

In a five-star restaurant recently, my husband wanted chips with his meal, but my daughter and I insisted that — because of our posh surroundings — he ask for 'French fries'.

Having taken our order, the waiter was then asked for a side order of French fries, to which he replied that he was sorry, they didn't have any — would chips do instead?!

Overheard by Anonymous, in a five-star restaurant, no less!
Posted on Monday, 6 August 2007

Scary

On the no. 130 bus home to Clontarf, some bird on her phone:

'Hiye, yea, listen we're goin' te Skerries ... no man, Skerries ... What d'ye mean? Can ye not hear me? SKERRIES! S. C. A. R. Y. S.'

I couldn't laugh at the time for fear of getting my head kicked in ...

Overheard by Josie, the no. 130 bus
Posted on Monday, 6 August 2007

Ryanair wit

Was on the plane home from Spain the other day.

As usual, at the end when we are waiting to get off the plane, the pilot's voice comes over the speakers, 'Thank you for flying Ryanair,' etc.

Just as we think he's finished, he comes out with this:

'... and it's very rainy in Dublin this evening. If you don't have an umbrella, you might need to contact Rihanna, and ask her for an umbrella, ella, ella.'

Certainly a break away from the usual, 'Flight time is two hours ...' etc.

Cheap flights, and a bit of humour: what more could you ask for!

Overheard by cc, Ryanair flight!
Posted on Sunday, 5 August 2007

Ballyer at Heathrow

I was going through Heathrow Airport a few years ago getting a connecting flight to the States. I got talking to a guy originally from Ballyfermot who now lived in New York.

He was a rough looking guy, and wasn't too fond of the British airport authorities.

Before going through customs he told me he could guarantee that they would stop and question him.

Apparently he was always stopped.

Anyway, we arrived at the part where they check

your passport and the airport customs guy asks in his finest English accent, 'Are we going anywhere nice today, Sir?'

The bloke from Ballyfermot replied,

'Well, I'm going somewhere nice, but I don't remember f**king inviting you anywhere!'

Overheard by Anonymous, Heathrow Airport
Posted on Saturday, 4 August 2007

At the cinema

Was at the cinema years ago when Jaws came out and at the start of the film the camera is in the water looking onto a quiet beach. It's moving back and forth, we see a young couple about to come in swimming and the Jaws music is playing. Not a sound out of anyone when we overhear a voice at the front, 'Jaysis how'd they get a fish to operate a camera?'

Overheard by Alan, cinema
Posted on Sunday, 4 August 2007

The magic word ...

My four-year-old sister was asking me to get her something (I forget what) and I said to her, 'What's the magic word?'

Sister: 'Abracadabra!'

Me: 'No, it starts with P. 'P–L ...'

Sister: 'Plabracadabra!'

I think she needs some lessons in manners ...

Overheard by CoolKitty, at home
Posted on Saturday, 4 August 2007

Orange juice and coffee — together at last

In Supermac's on O'Connell Street about three years ago, I was standing at the counter and the following conversation took place.

Customer: 'Hi, see this voucher I have, "Buy a burger and get a free 7Up"?'

Guy behind the counter: 'Yeah?'

Customer: 'Instead of a 7Up, can I get an orange juice?'

Supermac's Staff Kid: 'Yeah, okay.'

Customer: 'Great. Eh, instead of buying a burger, can I buy a coffee and still get the free 7Up?'

Supermac's staff kid: 'Hold on, I'll ask someone.'

(kid explains customer query to manager)

Supermac's manager (looking annoyed): 'Yeah, okay.'

Supermac's staff kid (to the customer): 'Do you want those in separate cups?'

Overheard by Neilo Indestructibloke,
Supermac's in O'Connell Street
Posted on Wednesday, 1 August 2007

Children of Lir ...

Two girls passed me by on O'Connell Street, obviously discussing a recent History class.

Girl 1: 'And they were changed back from swans after 900 years ...'

Girl 2: 'Nine hundred years? Jaysus, imagine waking up after nine hundred years ... sure you'd be f**ked!'

Overheard by Anonymous, O'Connell Street
Posted on Tuesday, 31 July 2007

Cinderella's fella

Standing outside Burger King on Grafton Street about four o'clock on a Sunday morning, one shoe in my hand because my feet were killing me. Lad wearing a white tracksuit, baseball cap, sovereigns comes up to me and asks me can he have my shoe.

'What do ya want my shoe for?' I said.

'So I can find ya in de mornin'!'

Overheard by Anonymous, Grafton Street
Posted on Tuesday, 31 July 2007

Wherever they may rome

Waiting for a few mates on Grafton Street on Friday night, two fairly posh girls in their mid 20s walking past:

Girl 1: 'Did you hear about that Roma family on the M50 roundabout? Terrible isn't it?'

Girl 2: 'I know!' (gasping) 'And I thought Italy was a developed country!'

Overheard by The Long Fellow, Grafton Street
Posted on Monday, 30 July 2007

The art of subtlety

At the hurling in Croker over the weekend. Walking up Clonliffe Road after the games. A garda sitting on a horse which was very well endowed. Lad about thirty yards away shouts up the road,

'Would ya look at the bollox on the horse!'

Overheard by Cyril sneer, Clonliffe Road
Posted on Sunday, 29 July 2007

The 78A to Outer Mongolia

On the no. 78A bus there was the usual group of skangers upstairs, one of them is talking (very loudly) about travelling.

Skanger 1: 'Ya know wha, you never really know anythin' about life until you've travelled.'

Skanger 2: 'Yeah, like what?'

Skanger 1: 'Ya know, like about how other people live and how different life is in other places, it opens your mind, ya know!'

Skanger 2: 'No way, and where did you go?'

Skanger 1: 'Torremolinos ... it's in Spain.'

I was half expecting her to say Outer Mongolia or something!

Overheard by Jenny, no. 78A bus
Posted on Tuesday, 24 July 2007

Smoke gets in your eyes

Overheard by a Dub in Atlanta.

Four middle-aged 'chandeliers' eating and drinking and smoking like troopers. Disgusted lady at the next table bursts out in an exasperated voice,

'Gentlemen, your cigarette smoke is really bothering me.'

'It's killing me!' said the oldest and most flamboyant.

Overheard by daddyo, Atlanta
Posted on Tuesday, 24 July 2007

The flying nuns

Not so much overheard as seen in Dublin.

My Nan got tickets at Christmas time for a hymn concert being given by the nuns. On the bottom of the ticket was,

'No moshing or crowd surfing.'

Need I say more ...

Overheard by Shedevil, my Nan's house
Posted on Monday, 23 July 2007

May cause drowsiness?

In a doctor's surgery with my three-year-old daughter.

Doctor: 'Give her one 5 ml spoonful three times a day before meals and don't let her operate a bicycle ...'

Overheard by Cal, doctor's surgery
Posted on Friday, 20 July 2007

The clap

As our plane taxied to a halt at Dublin Airport a couple of months ago, the passengers broke into a spontaneous round of applause. An old dear, seated beside a retired pilot, smiled knowingly at him and was heard to say,

'I'll bet you OFTEN got the clap!'

Overheard on a plane which had just landed at Dublin Airport
Posted on Friday, 20 July 2007

Colour-blind

Girl walking down O'Connell Street wearing a
purple and black stripey jumper. Scumbag
shouts over to her, 'Here, Missus, watcha tink ye
ar, a bee or somtin?!'

Overheard by botsy, O'Connell Street
Posted on Wednesday, 18 July 2007

An old excuse reworked

My friend walked into work a bit late one day
and said,

'Sorry I'm late, me dog ate me watch,' expecting
no one to believe him. Later on that day a
woman in the office came up to him and said in
a serious manner,

'Sorry to hear about your dog eating your watch,
was it expensive?'

Overheard by turbo, work
Posted on Wednesday, 18 July 2007

Good weekend

Heard a lad shout this out of his tent to
someone at the Oxegen festival:

'You can take me virginity, but yer not gettin' any
of me bleedin' cans!'

Overheard by Handbag, Oxegen
Posted on Tuesday, 17 July 2007

Pub crawl

A few years ago having a few drinks in the Stork pub on Cork Street, just two doors down from Morrissey's pub. Watching United against Blackburn. Blackburn go 2-0 up.

Not long after this a bloke walks in, looks up at the telly and says, 'Ahh, f**k this, I'm going back up to Morrissey's — its only 1-0 up there!'

Overheard by John, the Stork pub
Posted on Monday, 16 July 2007

Candid camera

Walking into Oxegen last week and in the car park there was the usual collection of vendors selling their wares. As we passed, a guy shouted out, 'Get your camerits,' much to the amusement of my English boyfriend. Just as we're about to crack up, another seller in front of us shouts out the same thing!

How do we explain where the 'its' came from?

Overheard by Anna, Oxegen festival car park
Posted on Monday, 16 July 2007

Selective sunshine

On the last proper day of glorious sunshine my girlfriend and I went to Donabate beach. We were lying in the sun when I heard this bickering beside me.

Girl 1: 'It's fucken freezen!'

Girl 2: 'Let's go to the other end of the beach, it's warmer!'

Girl 1: 'Why?'

Girl 2: 'Cuz the sun is shinen down there!'

Overheard by Alan, Donabate beach
Posted on Sunday, 15 July 2007

Cheap thrills

Overheard two lads working in a lift shaft, first lad had just got off the phone.

First Lad: 'That was me mate, d'ye wanna buy a rampant rabbit for yer moth? Only 30 quid!'

Second Lad: 'What, like to breed other rabbits?'

First Lad: 'What?'

Second Lad: 'Like a sex-mad rabbit?'

First Lad: 'Are you bleedin' serious?'

Overheard by sammy, on a site in Cookstown
Posted on Sunday, 15 July 2007

The new curate

Two ladies at the hairdressers, discussing the new foreign curate:

'Ah sure, he gives LOVELY sermons. It's just a pity you can't understand the half of them!'

Overheard by Anonymous, at the hairdressing salon
Posted on Saturday, 14 July 2007

The no. 145 bus ... you've gotta love it

Getting the no. 145 bus home from town last night around 11, there was four 'head the balls' on their way home, all drunk. There were three girls and one lad. One of the girls said to the fella, 'Wat were ya in fur?'

He replied, 'Aaarmed robbery 'n GBH.'

Her reply to that was, 'I don't mind a bit of greviouslee badily herm meself!'

Overheard by James, no. 145 bus
Posted on Friday, 13 July 2007

Explaining the complexities of life

English class and we were reading extracts from whatever novel we were studying, taking turns to read. One of the lads at the back, John, was daydreaming, but was interrupted by the teacher.

Teacher: 'John, what is love?'

John (in deep thought); 'Well, Miss, love is like when a man and a woman ...'

Teacher (interrupting): 'No, John, read the paragraph starting with "What is love?"'

Overheard by flanman, English class
Posted on Friday, 13 July 2007

Best excuse ever

Two years ago when I was in school, this guy, bit of a joker, saunters into French class half an hour late. The following conversation took place.

Teacher (in her French accent): 'Mark! Where have you been?'

Mark (strong Dublin accent): 'Eh, I was down in

Mr Darcy's (the principal) office.'

Teacher: 'Yes, Mark, I know that, I was down in Mr Darcy's office half an hour ago, he said he'd only keep you for ten minutes, that was half an hour ago, where have you been since?'

Mark: 'Eh, well I bumped into Keego on the way back ...'

Teacher: 'Yes, and ...?'

Mark: 'Ah, sure ya kno yourself when ya get chattin', Miss ...'

Classic!

Overheard by Dave, Institute of Education
Posted on Thursday, 12 July 2007

Francophilia

Three girls talking up their sexual experiences.

The 1st says she'd had a 'menage a twa'.

The 2nd asks what that is.

The 3rd says, 'It's French for a rendezvous between three people.'

Overheard by Tadaa!!!, on the no. 75 bus to Dun Laoghaire
Posted on Thursday, 12 July 2007

Politically incorrect

Two girls in work discussing refugees.

Girl 1: 'There's so many African-Americans in Dublin!'

Girl 2: 'African-Americans? That's not what you call black people!'

Girl 1: 'I thought that was the PC term.'

Girl 2: 'Only if they are American.'

Girl 1: 'Oh yeah, well there's so many African-American-Irish in Dublin.'

Overheard by Cal, work

Posted on Thursday, 12 July 2007

To court or Cork?

A couple of years ago when he was four, I asked my son if he would like to go to Cork on holidays. He looked at me with a horrified face and said, 'But I've been a good boy, why do I have to go to Cork?'

I was a little confused, so I asked him what was wrong and his answer was,

'All the bold people go to Cork and the judge bashes them with his hammer!'

Overheard by emmsy, at home

Posted on Tuesday, 10 July 2007

Spoonful of sugar

In Capitol last Friday night, heading upstairs, and this girl walks down the stairs, kind of big build, large chested, and we just hear a guy shout to his mate,

'Here, have ya got any Calpol? She's very chesty!'

Overheard by The Decadent Kids, Capitol

Posted on Monday, 9 July 2007

The dog's bollox

Last week my son turned around and said,

'Dad, now I know what those things are between Peanut's legs.' I looked at our West Highland Terrier, Peanut, who was lying on his back with his legs wide open.

'What are they?' I asked anticipating the answer. 'They're his balls,' he said with a grin. I smiled and said,

'That's right, they *are* his balls.' He looked at the dog and said,

'I used to think they were his brains!'

Overheard by Jay, at home
Posted on Sunday, 8 July 2007

Crash landing

Seen rather than heard.

Written on the emergency plastic card in the back sleeve of the seat on an Aer Lingus plane (the part where the man has his head bent down whilst holding on to the seat in front). Big speech bubble:

'OH SHIT!'

Overheard by Phil, Aer Lingus plane
Posted on Friday, 6 July 2007

D4 lad a little out of touch

I was walking down Baggot Street Lower outside the Bank of Ireland head office when I overheard one D4 lad say to the other country lad in a posh accent:

'Hey, do you want to go and get a few britneys (beers) after work?'

Country Lad: 'I'm headin' back home. I'm goin' baling.'

D4 Lad: 'What's baling? Is that a new water sport or something?'

Surprised, the country boy replied: 'Cutting the grass and putting it together.'

D4 Lad: 'Oh, does that still go on?'

Overheard by peter, Baggot Street Lower
Posted on Thursday, 28 June 2007

Election muddle

Heading home from work on the bus during the general election and there's a poster up of Noel Ahern (Bertie's brother).

Girl #1: 'Jaysus, Bertie looks completely different in his posters, doesn't he?'

Girl #2: 'That's his brother.'

Girl #1: 'No it's not, it says "Ahern" not "O'Hern" on it.'

Overheard by Ash, no. 17a bus Dublin
Posted on Monday, 25 June 2007

Not making a splash ...

In Briody's pub yesterday after the match, one of the kids was talking about scuba diving and asked us (quite loudly),

'Why do scuba divers always fall backwards off

the boat?' Before any of us could answer, one of the old pint-suppers pipes up — without even turning around from the bar,

'Because if they fell forwards they would still be on the boat!'

Overheard by peter, Briody's pub, Marlborough Street
Posted on Monday, 25 June 2007

Nobody Knows

On Hill 16 for the Dublin v Offaly Leinster semi-final. There was a minute's silence for a recently deceased GAA member. About 40 seconds into the minute's silence, some wise-crack said,

'I DON'T KNOW WHAT A TRACKER MORTGAGE IS ...'

Overheard by Alan, Hill 16, Dublin match
Posted on Monday, 25 June 2007

Joining in the festivities

I decided to check out Gay Pride on Saturday. I have a new camera, and I wanted to get some practice with it. These two blokes approached me, a bit of a smell of drink off them, but in good form.

'We want to be on the front page of the *Irish Times* — take our photo!'

I played along. They invited one of their female friends to join them in the picture, and I took a picture of the three of them, one of the blokes giving the other a kiss on the cheek. I showed them the photo.

'Eh, we're just in town for the day — what's this parade about?'

Overheard by Anonymous, Parnell Square East, just before the start of the Gay Pride parade

Posted on Monday, 25 June 2007

Here comes trouble ...

A few years back I was walking through a north Dublin housing estate where I saw two women talking at a gate. A young fella walked out of the house and passed the women. Without stopping the conversation, one of the women slapped the young fella on the back of the head as he passed.

Young Fella: 'Wha was dat for?'

Woman: 'You're either coming from trouble or goin' to it so you deserve a clip round the ear for whatever you done, or whatever you're about to do!'

Young Fella: 'Ah, Maaaaaaaaaaa!'

Overheard by Anonymous, De North Side
Posted on Thursday, 21 June 2007

Tinky Winky goes to the deed poll office

Babysitting my friend's little girl the other day (she's two) and she sat down to watch Teletubbies. She was telling me all about them, so I asked her what their names were. Apparently they're now called Po, Dipsy, Lala and Winky Wanky!

Overheard by Anonymous, my friend's house
Posted on Thursday, 21 June 2007

They'll take your job next ...

St Patrick's Day 2004, my brother and I were going to the airport to meet our Mam who'd been away. We got a taxi, and in conversation with the driver we somehow got onto the fact that our President, Mary McAleese, is from the six counties.

Some time later, conversation got round to the long fellow, Eamon De Valera, who was Spanish/American.

Sometime after that, we got round to St Patrick, who was Welsh.

The taxi driver said, 'Typical, all the good jobs are taken by foreigners!'

Overheard by FrankO, taxi to Dublin Airport
Posted on Wednesday, 20 June 2007

Flirtatious in a sober drunk way

Girl 1 (to drunk friend): 'Oh my God, you are so drunk. Stop behaving like you did out there!'

Drunk Girl: 'What? I wasn't behaving? What do you mean?'

Girl 1: 'Seriously, you were rubbing your crotch against that guy over there!'

Drunk Girl: 'I was NOT! I am almost sober.'

Girl 1: 'Aaah yea! Your crotch was ALL over him. You wouldn't do that if you were sober!'

Drunk Girl: 'I totally would!'

Overheard by Anonymous, toilets at Quays Bar
Posted on Tuesday, 19 June 2007

Eye and Ear

Driving past the Eye and Ear Hospital a few years ago, my mate goes,

'Jaysus that must be a mad job to have, being one of them eyeaneers.' Confused by this, I asked him to explain himself.

'Ya know, eyeaneers, them fellas that look after your eyes.'

He thought they were like engineers! All his life he genuinely thought that!

Overheard by stevo, passing the Eye and Ear Hospital
Posted on Tuesday, 19 June 2007

Health warning

Cheeky young professional type passes a kid of about 15 with his back to a wall smoking a cigarette and says, 'Smoking's bad for your health!'

Quick as a flash the kid says, in a thick Dublin accent, 'Yeh, so's bein' a bollix.'

Overheard by Colm, Aungier Street
Posted on Monday, 18 June 2007

Life's questions

One night, we stopped off in Blackrock for chips on the way home. While I was in the chipper, handbags erupted on the street between a few south-Dublin types. Ralph Lauren, Hugo Boss and Henry Lloyd had never seen the like. It was fairly harmless stuff.

Anyway, I joined the gallery of gawkers outside, enjoying the entertainment while eating our chips. A taxi pulled up, and from the doorway of Tonic Bar tottered two gorgeous young wans, all boob tubes, glamour and mini-skirts. The lads' attention was drawn away from the minor scuffle as they all stared in awe at the visions of beauty to our left.

The guy beside me, who was a few pints in, with a chip hovering close to his lips, nudged me gently and said,

'Jazes, how would you be gay?'

Overheard by Murray, outside the Central Café, Blackrock
Posted on Monday, 18 June 2007

Dub abroad

While boarding a plane in Lanzarote, I observed a man mid 50s, very tanned from his holiday, bright yellow polo shirt, a sovereign ring on almost every finger and a very strong Dublin accent. He's walking down towards his seat with his bags when he recognises someone from home.

'Ah Jaysus, Jim, howsagoin? Yis have a bleedin' great colour — were ya away or wha?'

Overheard by Pongo, in Lanzarote while boarding the plane back to Dublin

Posted on Monday, 18 June 2007

Great nickname

Couple of young wans on the back of the no. 75 bus. They're talking loudly about a porno movie they saw the other night. Conversation goes like this:

Girl 1: 'Da noises she was makin', all dat moanin', dat was mad, like.'

Girl 2: 'Wot was mad bout it?'

Girl 1: 'Do you ever make noises like dat when you're doin' it?'

Girl 2 (very proud): 'Jaysus, they don't call me 'Emer the Screamer' for nuthin!'

Overheard by Anonymous, no. 75 bus

Posted on Friday, 15 June 2007

Even the teacher creased herself laughing

Very boring Leaving Cert English class many years ago.

Teacher (reading from novel): 'They were proud people, they stood erect and stiff ...'

(Shouted from back of class): 'They were a shower of pricks ...'

Overheard by Ted, English class
Posted on Thursday, 14 June 2007

Culture shock

Waiting for the back door of a Ryanair plane to open (people all standing at their seats with bags in hands), a man turns round and says to an Asian man in the seat behind him (who he obviously knew),

'Hey, Mahmood, I was just thinking sometimes it's great to be a Pakistani!'

'Why's that?' says Mahmood.

'Cos ye nearly always get a whole row of seats to yer self!'

The look of shocked faces was priceless — until the two of them laughed!

Overheard by Paul, Ryanair plane
Posted on Wednesday, 13 June 2007

Nature calls ... at Clery's

I was waiting for a taxi on O'Connell Street one night when I noticed a group of three girls. Two of them were dressed well, but the third ruined the image by shouting,

'I'm goin' fer a piiiiss!'

She marches up the steps next to Clery's and hoists up her skirt and pulls down her knickers. Next thing you hear is her screeching,

'F**k off! F**k off! I've a bladder infection!' at a passer-by.

Then she strolls down the steps, fixing her skirt and pulling up her knickers on the way down, and announces loudly,

'I'm going for a box of faaaags!' marching off, looking like a man, leaving the other two looking at each other in horror and disbelief.

Overheard by RandomMan, the steps beside Clery's
Posted on Wednesday, 13 June 2007

Members only

Queuing outside a night-club in Temple Bar. Two likely lads ahead of me were swaying gently from side to side. 'Are yiz members?' asks the bouncer.

'We are,' say the lads.

'I'm sorry, then. It's non-members night only!'

Overheard by Jimbo, Temple Bar
Posted on Tuesday, 12 June 2007

Objection to licence renewal

Work canteen (yonks ago), a news report comes on the radio saying how River Phoenix has died following a 'lethal cocktail' of drink and drugs.

Up pipes one lad: 'Jayus, that's terrible, they shouldn't be allowed to serve them.'

'Serve what?'

'Them lethal cocktails — they're always killing people.'

... back to quietly munching our sangers ...

Overheard by Anonymous, canteen in Tallaght factory
Posted on Sunday, 10 June 2007

On tow

A few years ago our car engine blew up. I was on maternity leave at the time so I was too broke to pay for the breaker's yard. It just sat in our garden for about a month with a big 'On Tow' sign in the back window.

One day a Traveller called to the door and asked, 'Is tha' a "For Sale" sign on the car?'

I didn't have the heart to tell him, so I said the car was wrecked but he could have it ... bless.

Overheard by Cal, my house
Posted on Friday, 8 June 2007

I know a little Latin ...

Getting off the ferry in Dun Laoghaire after a fairly rough crossing from Holyhead:

Auld Wan 1: 'That was a bit rough.'

Auld Wan 2: 'Yeah, it's nice to be back on terra cotta.'

Overheard by John, Dun Laoghaire ferry terminal
Posted on Friday, 8 June 2007

Getting on the property ladder ...

In a friend of a friend's house, queuing for a sunbed session.

Girl 1: 'It's my 21st next month, I hope you're all coming.'

Girl 2: 'You're 21 already. And you've no kids yet?'

Girl 1: 'No, why?'

Girl 2: 'Well, how the f**k are you going to get a house?'

Overheard by Barb, The Wild West (Dublin 22)
Posted on Thursday, 7 June 2007

This was on the first pint!

Watching the news a few months ago in the pub, the reporter says, 'Now over to our correspondent in Paris.' The French reporter gave his report in English.

My mate said, 'Isn't it good the way they put on the accent no matter where they are reporting from?'

I asked him to explain — kind of hoping he was joking!

He thought it was an *English* reporter putting on a *French* accent, rather than a *French* reporter speaking *English*.

I actually didn't laugh at first! I just sat there thinking — this guy has been thinking this all his life! Every time he has watched a report from anywhere, he has thought some English guy was in that country mimicking their accents!

Overheard by Fran, Pub
Posted on Tuesday, 5 June 2007

Treated like royals

Walking along the road out of Croke Park after the Dublin v Meath match. Heard this gathering phlegm and spit noise behind me. I stopped, checked my jacket, and looked beside me to see a little Dub about seven or eight.

He says, 'Don't worry, I was aiming at that Meath fella ahead. It landed on him! Sure I wouldn't do any harm to a Dub!'

Nice!

Overheard by gormdubhgorm, walking from
Croke Park near Clonliffe House
Posted on Monday, 4 June 2007

Dah's great valu, wah!

Standing having a smoke on North Earl Street, overheard the following:

Fundraiser: 'Hiya, how's it going? You couldn't spare a minute for Concern, please?'

Dub Fella (mate beside him): 'Yeh, gowan, make it bleedin' quick wil yeh.'

Fundraiser (launches into speech, then she says): 'Did you know you can feed an entire family for a month for €21 in Darfur?'

Dub Fella: 'F**kin' jazis, dah's greight value, wah! I shud bleedin' muave der!'

The poor girl actually looked really amused! I think she was glad of a unique response for a change!

Overheard by doyler, North Earl Street
Posted on Friday, 1 June 2007

Watch out for toilet trickery!

While sitting on the toilet in work one afternoon, I began reading the graffiti on the door! Here someone had written, 'Do you want to play toilet tennis?'

Pondering the question I thought, 'Yes!' and read on.

It said, 'Look left', which I happily proceeded to do; it then directed me to, 'Look right', which I also did. Reading on, I continued following the same directions! It was only after 4-love that I realised I'd been had!

Overheard by Mick, Smyths Toys, Tallaght
Posted on Thursday, 31 May 2007

Long-distance runner

Some time ago I was running alone in the Phoenix Park. I saw this lone runner, head down, running hard, coming towards me. When he was just about to pass me and without stopping, he asked in his best Dub accent out of the side of his mouth,

'Are them f***ing Kenyans far behind me?'

All I could do was smile and said to myself,
'Good one!'

Overheard by Duggie, Phoenix Park
Posted on Wednesday, 30 May 2007

Raking it on the 77

Decided to be brave last night by getting the no.
77 bus home from town. At Cork Street, a
rough-looking guy ('a skanger' to be politically
incorrect) gets on carrying a garden rake.

As he takes his seat upstairs he announces to
everybody: 'If any of yous make a rake joke
you'll get it in de head.'

That bus never ceases to amaze me.

Overheard by G, no. 77 bus
Posted on Wednesday, 30 May 2007

Dope caught in the headlights

One of my colleagues came into work late one
day with this excuse:

'My car wouldn't start this morning. The
battery wasted because my electricity went last

night so I used the headlights to light up the
front room ...'

Overheard by Count Cockula, in work
Posted on Tuesday, 29 May 2007

The voice of reason!

Sitting at my desk at work, another quiet and
boring day in the office ... just getting on with it
as you do.

My Colleague (sitting opposite me): 'Would you
ever shut the f**k up!'

Me: 'But ... I didn't say anything!'

My Colleague: 'Not you! The voices in my feckin'
head!'

I have since moved desks ...

Overheard by SA-Tam, in the office
Posted on Monday, 28 May 2007

Ello, ello, ello

My friend (who is a bit of a smart ass) was
stopped for speeding on the Navan Road.

Cop: 'I've been waiting for you all day!'

Friend: 'I know, I got here as quick as I could!'

Overheard by Marty, Navan Road
Posted on Monday, 28 May 2007

The future is healthy

Son: 'I want tea.'

Mother (who had just ordered coffee): 'Yer not

gettin' tea, it's bad for ye ... yer getting a Coke.'

Overheard by Anonymous, Café Sofia, Wexford Street

Posted on Monday, 28 May 2007

Cheap burial

My Dad ordered a skip a couple of weeks ago and rounded up a couple of my brothers to help him move the stuff into it (trees, a shed, rubbish). Two days before the skip arrives one of my brothers rings my Dad and the conversation goes like this:

Brother: 'Da, I have a bit of a problem.'

Da: 'Wha, son?'

Brother: 'Well, ya know the way you're after getting a skip? Mrs X just died so I'm in a bit of a pickle.' (meaning he couldn't help cause he had to go to his close friend's funeral)

Da: 'Well, like, I'd love to help ya, son, but I'm sorry, the skip is gonna be full up as it is, so there will be no room for her in it.'

Very insensitive — but also very funny at the time!

Overheard by Anonymous, at home

Posted on Monday, 28 May 2007

Hurt in the fracas

Grafton Street, one of our friends was caught in the crossfires of a bit of a mêlée. The Garda came and were looking for witnesses and statements. They asked my friend, 'Were you also hurt in the fracas?' He answered:

'I don't know where my fracas is — but my lip is all bleedin'.'

Overheard by Derek, Dublin late at night
Posted on Sunday, 27 May 2007

Find X

Well, not so much overheard ...

On our really important end-of-year exams, one of the Maths questions was a triangle with lots of angles marked on. The instruction for the question was 'Find X' (you were obviously meant to calculate angle X).

However, one of the guys in my class simply drew a circle around X and wrote, 'Here it is!'

Classic!

Overheard by CoolKitty, school
Posted on Saturday, 26 May 2007

Broken clouds

Pilot giving his spiel before take-off, Aer Arann, Dublin to Kerry:

'The weather in Kerry is similar to here, 15 degrees, light winds with broken clouds, though we hope to have the clouds fixed by the time we arrive.'

Overheard by Kevin, Aer Arann flight, Dublin Airport
Posted on Friday, 25 May 2007

Kissing rules

Walking around an estate, I overheard two little boys talking about girls. They were about eight.

Boy 1: 'Do you two kiss? You have to kiss your girlfriend like a million times before you get married. And then once a day when you're married.'

Boy 2: 'No, twice a day. One when the husband comes home from work and one when you're in bed.'

Boy 1: 'Oh, and one when the wife gets home ...'

Overheard by Lauren, Shankill
Posted on Friday, 25 May 2007

I love the respect my boyfriend has for me ...

I'm a scouser and when I was working in Italy my Dubliner boyfriend was over to visit me. We were having a lock-in in the bar where I worked and my boss was telling us a delightful story about when he had crabs!

So, he was explaining all about the creatures and then stated, 'The female crabs are actually born pregnant.'

Quick as a flash my boyfriend asked, 'What, like scousers?!'

Overheard by slick, bar in Italy, with Dubliner
Posted on Thursday, 24 May 2007

Pyjama party

Overseen not overheard.

While queuing to cast my vote in the general election today at St Attracta's National School polling station, I couldn't believe my eyes.

Two girls about 20 years old in front of me in the queue — both wearing PINK PYJAMAS!

Absolutely no shame! I wish I had my camera phone.

Overheard by Vinny, St Attracta's school, Dundrum
Posted on Thursday, 24 May 2007

Great comeback

A bus stops with its front wheels slightly inside a yellow box at a junction. A guy with a flash girlfriend and a flash convertible car pulls up beside the bus.

The flash guy shouts out his window at the bus driver,

'Yellow box, yellow box!'

The bus driver opens his window and says back to him,

'You'd better get her to the clinic!'

Overheard by Anonymous, junction on Malahide Road
Posted on Thursday, 24 May 2007

The Mile High club

Recently got a flight to the UK. The pilot came on board to say the usual, introducing himself etc. He finished by saying,

'Hope you enjoy the flight, have a drink, relax, listen to some music, or feel the leg of the person sitting next to you ...'

Put everyone on the plane in a good mood for the rest of the flight!

Overheard by Sarah, Aer Lingus flight
Posted on Thursday, 24 May 2007

Times are hard

Was waiting at the pedestrian crossing at College Green last week. Nice sunny day, a gush of people waiting to cross.

A taxi pulls up at the lights (2004 BMW 5 series), driver's arm hanging out the window. Lad shouts over to him,

'No money in taxiing, eh? ME BOLLIX!'

Overheard by Bazmo, College Green
Posted on Tuesday, 22 May 2007

The smoking ban in Dublin

Not overheard but overseen.

Outside the Coombe Hospital while walking in to visit a family member. Along the wall, two big 'No Smoking' signs, and below them were two wall-mounted ashtrays!

Overheard by Anonymous, Coombe
Posted on Monday, 21 May 2007

Smokey & the Bandit

On the Westport to Dublin train recently. The train was just pulling out of Tullamore when the driver came on the intercom to make the normal announcement in a real Dublin accent:

'Could I have your attention, please! Would the person with their arm out the window drop the cigarette ... next stop Portarlington.'

Overheard by indcar, Westport to Dublin train
Posted on Monday, 21 May 2007

A hard case of the Ballymun Blues

A few years ago a friend of ours was bragging about the new hard-shelled guitar case he had just bought. He was telling us about how it was so strong that ... 'You can climb to the top of the Ballymun towers, drop it off the edge and it wouldn't break when it hits the ground.'

My friend chirps in:

'Yeah, maybe you're right, but I betcha it wouldn't be there when ya get back down.'

Overheard by Derek, Dublin pub
Posted on Friday, 18 May 2007

Bus to the moon

I got on a no. 83 bus just at the top of Booterstown Avenue. I was a bit tired so I checked whether the bus went to Stillorgan. The smug, sunglass-wearing, ridiculous moustached, angry bus-driver replied,

'No! It goes to the f**kin' moon!'

Wanted to reply, 'One to the moon, please,' but his tattooed knuckles said not to.

Thanks, Dublin Bus.

Overheard by Ian, no. 83 bus
Posted on Thursday, 17 May 2007

Xenophobia on the Luas

Three French tourists were on the Luas from Tallaght. Every time we stopped, they mimicked the Irish translation of the stations.

Voice: 'The Four Courts ... Na Ceithre Cúirteanna.'

Frenchie 1: 'Naccera corchinna.' (laughs)

Dub: 'I'd like to see yis laugh if the next stop was Darndale, ya frogs!'

Overheard by Sam, Luas from Tallaght
Posted on Wednesday, 16 May 2007

Full-time bus driver and part-time comedian

Getting on a bus in Crumlin, a would-be passenger enquires of the driver,

Woman: 'Do you go to the shopping centre in Tallaght?'

Driver: 'No, love, I normally shop locally.'

Overheard by Richie, Crumlin, on a no. 77 bus
Posted on Sunday, 13 May 2007

Doing a domestic

Was out shopping with a mate yesterday, buying stacks of cleaning equipment. Leaving the shop, an aul' one turns and asks, 'Doing a bit of cleaning, lads?'

Quick as a flash my buddy turns and says, 'Nah, it's my girlfriend's birthday!'

The look on the aul' one's face — classic!

Overheard by BB, Bakers Corner
Posted on Thursday, 12 April 2007

All he could do was laugh

At work in the local factory today we were all sitting down waiting for work to finish. The boss comes by and notices a lad at the end of the line not doing anything, so he shouts over, 'Here, wot dya call this?' then points to his imaginary watch.

The young lad replies, 'Yer wrist?'

Overheard by Stevie, factory in Monkstown
Posted on Friday, 11 May 2007

Not quite the charitable type ...

Having left Eason's on O'Connell Street, I turned right towards Grafton Street.

I noticed a stereotypical northsider talking to one of those chuggers from Concern or somewhere. Passed just in time to hear him say,

'Wha? Jaze, I thought youz were gonna give ME money! Forget it, pal!'

Overheard by Jonny, O'Connell Street
Posted on Thursday, 10 May 2007

Tackling the matter

Sitting in the stand in front of two archetypical middle-aged Dubs at a recent soccer match in Richmond Park, I was privy to their debate regarding a particularly aggressive midfielder who was playing at the time.

'Sure, he'd break yer leg,' exclaimed one of the men, disgusted. His friend reflected for at moment on the accusation.

'He would not,' he calmly disagreed, 'He'd break yer *two* legs.'

Overheard by Odd Slob, Richmond Park
Posted on Wednesday, 9 May 2007

Labour

I was coming home from Skerries when I saw an election poster for the Labour Party. It had been vandalised with the usual stuff (goatie, glasses, etc.) But in a speech bubble it said,

'Help, I'm in Labour!'

Overheard by Brian, on the road from Skerries to Rush
Posted on Monday, 7 May 2007

She's no good ...

Overheard in Fallon & Byrne recently, man with English accent talking into mobile:

'... and the worst thing is, she doesn't drink at all, so she remembers all my lies!'

Overheard by nefariousfaery, Fallon & Byrne, Exchequer Street
Posted on Sunday, 6 May 2007

Could only be said by a Dub

Guy: 'I hit him so hard on the top of his head, I broke his bleedin' ankles.'

Overheard by francy, on the no. 19 bus
Posted on Saturday, 5 May 2007

Bring on the exams!

I was in Biology class in sixth year and we were talking about the eye, as part of our revision for the Leaving Cert.

Our Teacher: 'What happens to our eyes when it gets dark?'

Student (deadly serious): 'Your night-vision comes on.'

Overheard by Lauren, Tallaght Community School
Posted on Wednesday, 2 May 2007

Tabloid Talk

Two women talking about Posh and Becks' move to LA:

Woman #1: 'Jayus, when they go over there, the pavarotti will be all over them!'

Woman #2: 'The what?'

Woman #1: 'You know, the newspaper people that follow you around!'

Overheard by Anonymous, pub in Portobello
Posted on Wednesday, 2 May 2007

Croker joker

Coming out of Croke Park a couple of years ago after a Dublin and Kildare match, the usual after-match crowds not moving very much. Then over the banter comes a shout,

'Don't mind those bleedin' traffic lights up there — keep on movin'!'

Overheard by wolftone, Croke Park
Posted on Tuesday, 1 May 2007

Sayin' me prayers

Run up to Christmas, Arnotts, busy. Long queues to pay. I come to the top of the queue with my presents. There are two women at the desk. The first (quite young) wrapping and calling out the items, the second (middle aged) keying the necessary into the cash register. Conversation as follows:

Young One: 'Four Galway crystal tumblers.'

Auld One: 'Wha? Will ya speak up so I can ear ye.'

Young One: 'I said four Galway crystal tumblers. Can't help it; I got a sore throat.'

Auld One: 'What's dat to me? How'd ye ge dat? Down on your knees again?'

Young One: 'Yea, sayin' me prayers.'

And they carried on without blinking an eye.

Overheard by Thomas, Arnotts
Posted on Monday, 30 April 2007

Warranty? Yeah right!

I was walking down O'Connell Street last week on a fine sunny day and stopped at a stall where this bloke was selling knock-off designer sunglasses. A young lad about 12 comes up to the guy and says,

'Hey, Mister, I bought these glasses about 20 minutes ago and they are way too big, do ya have any smaller ones?'

The bloke replied, 'Jung fella, it's not smaller glasses ya need, it's a bigger f**kin' head — now piss off!'

Overheard by bob, O'Connell Street
Posted on Monday, 30 April 2007

DART darlings

Heading to town on the DART on a Saturday evening, two D4 girls having a chat:

Girl #1: 'I mean I already pay, like, €50 a week rent, and I mean I only have one meal a day there and, loike, just sleep there, and he asked me for another €20? I couldn't believe it — I mean I only earn €500 a week you know?'

Girl #2: 'Oh my god, that's so unfair, my Dad wouldn't even ask me for money for anything ...'

Good to see these girls are prepared for the big bad world!

Overheard by Anonymous, the DART
Posted on Monday, 30 April 2007

Anto at the panto

At a pantomime in the Gaiety a few years ago with the family, and the usual scene happens where the villain creeps up on the star of the show. All the kids are screaming the whereabouts of the bad guy, when the kid sitting next to us gets into it, and starts shouting

'He's ahind ya, he's bleedin' ahind ya!'

Overheard by Derek, Gaiety Theatre Panto
Posted on Monday, 30 April 2007

Sore head

Waiting in the check-in queue in Manchester Airport for a flight back to Dublin, a Sikh was in front of us, wearing traditional turban. Young Dublin boy around six or seven shouts out,

'Dad, I really hope that man's head gets better soon.'

Innocence of kids …

Overheard by Anonymous, Manchester Airport
Posted on Monday, 30 April 2007

Go home ya culchie

Walking down Grafton Street one day, an old man (in his 80s at least!) starts singing at the top of his voice,

'TAKE ME HOME THE COUNTRY ROOOAD TO THE PLACE I KNOW BEST'

And next thing a skanger shouts across at him …

'Well then go home ya bleedin' culchie, we'd be better off without your bleedin' howlin'.'

The man quickly replies,

'Who the f**k are you callin' a culchie? I was born and bred on that road down there!'

Only in Dublin …

Overheard by Kaz, Grafton Street
Posted on Sunday, 29 April 2007

Selfish society

Girl: 'Spare a minute for Concern?'

Guy: 'Sorry, I'm not concerned.'

Overheard by Jay, bottom of Grafton Street
Posted on Sunday, 29 April 2007

Chocolate muffin!

My Mum comes back from Dunnes after doing the weekly shopping. She'd bought chocolate muffins for my brother as a treat.

She brings a muffin in to my brother and says,

'Stick your teeth into that big brown muff.'

Needless to say, my brother and I were speechless!

Overheard by Shelly, at home!
Posted on Saturday, 28 April 2007

Clothing has no morals these days!

'Jaysus the prices of these T-shirts here, they bleedin' rape your pocket!'

Overheard by Geraldine, clothes shop, Temple Bar
Posted on Saturday, 28 April 2007

Evolution in the social conduct of the no. 50 bus

I overheard an interesting conversation.

Person #1: 'Well, I am a little stuck for money at

the moment and this sounds like expensive stuff, besides getting needles and all!'

Person #2: 'Come on, we can share a needle then.'

Overheard by Even, de 50 out'ta tallah!
Posted on Saturday, 28 April 2007

A Ryanair welcome to Dublin!

Ryanair flight from Lubeck to Dublin. I'm sitting at the window. Coming in to land there's turbulence, fog — you name it. Very bumpy.

After a rough landing, genuinely relieved pilot announces over the intercom, 'Clear of the active runway, sir, thank f**k, I hadn't a clue where I was going ...'

Fifteen seconds later ...

'My apologies there, ladies and gentlemen, I, errrrr ...' (pause)

Fifteen seconds later ...

Other pilot: 'Ladies and gentlemen, welcome to Dublin!'

Overheard by Anonymous, Ryanair flight
Posted on Friday, 27 April 2007

Ditzy Dublin blondes

Guy says to friend, 'Oh, I saw your twin today!'

Friend says, 'Oh, really? What did she look like?'

Testament to think before you speak!

Overheard by Anonymous, in the ATM queue
Posted on Friday, 27 April 2007

Compassionate Kid

We had a group of kids, about 10 years of age, making their way into one of the buildings at DCU. As I started walking through the automatic revolving door, one of the kids hit the big red 'emergency stop' button at his side. The door came to a stand-still with me 'trapped' halfway around, between the two panes of glass.

Rather than just push the door, I start clutching my throat and pretend to be choking, dropping to my knees, giving it an Oscar-winning performance. Some of the kids started laughing, others weren't quite sure if I was joking or not, when suddenly the child who hit the button in the first place walks up to the glass, presses his face against it so I can hear, and shouts:

'Ah, will ye ever ge' outta dat, ya bollix!'

I laughed myself to tears.

Overheard by Fred, DCU Research Building
Posted on Friday, 27 April 2007

Behave

I was in a supermarket and a kid was running around and getting in other people's way. The mother looked at the kid and said,

'I have two words for you: Bee Haaave'

Needless to say, the child didn't behave at all!

Overheard in Tesco, Stillorgan
Posted on Friday, 27 April 2007

Mother's advice

On a DART, overheard a snippet of a conversation.

Guy #1: 'It's times like this that I wish I had listened to what my mother said.'

Guy #2: 'Well, what did she say?'

Guy #1: 'I have no idea — I didn't listen to her.'

Overheard by Anonymous, DART
Posted on Friday, 27 April 2007

I can't believe I said that!

At my brother's wedding some years ago. Towards the end of the mass the congregation was invited up to receive communion. It had been a while for me, but I went and did my duty. As the priest said, 'Body of Christ', I said, 'Oh, cheers — thanks!'

Overheard by Anonymous, church
Posted on Thursday, 26 April 2007

The Dublin mating ritual

I was walking through a car park outside a newsagents in the humble area of Coolock. There were two separate groups of about 10 people, one all girls and one all guys between 12 and 14. As I walked past the girls I heard one of them shout over to the group of guys,

'Here, will ANY of yous meet ANY of us?'

Overheard by Beddy, Coolock village
Posted on Thursday, 26 April 2007

Good manners

Standing in the ATM queue in college one day,
there was a girl in front of me taking out money.
The machine seemed to be taking its time giving
the money and she was looking around blankly,
as if off in her own world. Eventually, the money
comes out and she takes it, saying to the ATM,
'Thank you!'

Overheard by Elmo, UCD
Posted on Wednesday, 25 April 2007

Great answer

A few years back, we were in Biology class of
adolescent 14-year-old boys, dissecting insects.
The teacher asked, 'Can anyone tell us the
difference between the male and female stick
insect?'

Quick as a flash, the class wag pipes up with,

'Miss, the male has a bit more stick!'

Overheard by Mick, school
Posted on Wednesday, 25 April 2007

I spy with my little eye something beginning with IDIOT!

I was waiting at the bus stop at Eden Quay. A
group of girls started playing 'I Spy' to pass the
time.

Girl #1: 'I spy with my little eye, something
beginning with E.'

Girl #2: 'Eroplane!'

Overheard by Anonymous, Eden Quay

Posted on Tuesday, 24 April 2007

Bogger in sauna

In the sauna in DCU after soccer. This guy we know from Clare came in and sat down the front. He started to get a bit agitated, and after about five minutes jumped up and said to us,

'Jaysus Christ, lads, can we open the door — it's f**kin' roastin' in here ...'

Overheard by TP, DCU sports centre

Posted on Saturday, 21 April 2007

Where women never look!

In the pub with my brother-in-law discussing my sister's birthday and the cake. I asked where he would hide it so she wouldn't find it, to which he responded, 'In the oven, sure she'll never look in there.'

I fell over with laughter — and that's exactly where he hid it!

Overheard by Surprise Surprise, pub in Dublin 9

Posted on Thursday, 19 April 2007

I thought they only came out at night

Driving to work the other morning on a sunny day, I was stopped in traffic just outside my area. A car on the other side of the road drove by and I beeped to a friend of mine, who waved back.

As I went to drive off, my passenger door opened and a lad in site gear went to step in. We looked at each other, he turned and said,

'Ah shite, I thought you were me mate, sorry bud,' and as he was closing the door I heard him under his breath say to himself,

'For f**k's sake, John, you're only out of bed and you're embarrassing yourself.'

I laughed all the way to work!

Overheard by ST, old airport road
Posted on Thursday, 19 April 2007

Erecting the Spire

Back some time ago, I was observing the Spire in its earliest stages of construction, the first section having being just slotted into position.

The middle-aged man beside me was unimpressed,

'Isn't very big.'

To which his more optimistic friend replied,

'Wait till it gets horny ...'

Overheard by Odd Slob, O'Connell Street
Posted on Wednesday, 18 April 2007

Nelson for the Aras?

Was on the no. 10 bus to work, which also goes to Phoenix Park. Anyway about 20 proper 'langers' from Cork in their teens got on the bus and headed straight for the back seat, full of joy and excitement. One of them made a comment about someone famous living in the Phoenix Park but they couldn't remember who it was.

A reply came from one of them, 'Ah yea, it's your man, what's his name, that guy Mandela!'

'Oh yea,' they all said in agreement. Except for one of them.

She then confronted them: 'Will yas don't be stupid, it's the president fella, Bertie O'Hern!'

I wanted to jump out the window ...

Overheard by Anonymous, no. 10 bus
Posted on Wednesday, 18 April 2007

Cuisine de Dunnes

I was walking past an older couple in the supermarket the other day. As I was passing, the man turned to his wife and said, 'Cock oven?'

'Coq Au Vin!' replied his wife with a sigh.

Overheard by Peter, Dunnes Stores, St Stephen's Green
Posted on Wednesday, 18 April 2007

Too much time to think

A load of D4 heads on the way to Dundrum.

D4 #1: 'Oh my God, like, how do we know it's Tuesday? It could be Saturday or something?

Like, what do days go by?'

D4 #2: 'You're such an idiot, it goes by the sea!'

The rest all agree ...

Overheard by Kate, the bus to Dundrum
Posted on Tuesday, 17 April 2007

Charm school dropout

In a taxi on my way to work after a particularly hard night, I told the taxi man I was feeling a bit rough. 'Oh,' he says, 'you've no need to tell me, I can see it.' Deciding to take it in the humour that (hopefully) it was meant, I laughed. Then he says,

'Ah jaysus, love, I didn't mean to offend you there. I know you're laughing and all, but I know you're offended really. I know the way you women work — I was married to a pig in lipstick for twenty years!'

I wonder why the marriage hadn't worked out!

Overheard by Anonymous, in a taxi in Dublin
Posted on Tuesday, 17 April 2007

Our future sports stars!

Umpiring at the back of the goals at a GAA match last night and all the play was at one end of the pitch. The two corner backs, bored to tears, were just passing time talking to each other when one says to the other,

'Jaysus, I hope that f**king ball doesn't come down here, I can't run for shite.'

The other one replies, 'You'd want to give up them smokes then wouldn't ya?'

They were 12-year-old girls!

Overheard by Gerry, at a GAA match in Dublin
Posted on Tuesday, 17 April 2007

Head wrecker

Two women were talking together in a café on Thomas Street. One of the women's little boy started getting fidgety and wanted to leave. He kept pestering his mother to go until she lost her patience and turned to yell at him to shut up. Then she turned back to her friend and said,

'Jayzus, that fella would give a bleedin' Anadin a headache!'

Overheard by clio, a café on Thomas Street
Posted on Tuesday, 17 April 2007

The good auld days ...

This happened Saturday night, standing waiting to use the urinal while it was being used by my Dad and another man. Both of them are doing their business and the man next to him started talking:

'I remember the days when you were able to use the underground toilets in O'Connell Street. You'd go down, do your business and no one would bother you.'

My Dad agrees and then the man pointed over to one of the toilet attendants and said in a very

loud voice, 'Now you can't walk into the toilet
without them wanting to wipe your arse!'

Life's a beach and then you die ...

Woman on a packed train to her friend:

'Oh, I love dolphins, we saw one when we were
on holidays last summer. It was beached, but we
took some photos anyway ...'

Tinted windows

Went for a spin with a friend of mine who had
just bought a new car. My (blonde) friend was
sitting in the passenger seat and had bought a
new pair of sunglasses that day. She turns to my
friend who's driving and asks in all sincerity, 'Are
your windows tinted?'

We all burst out laughing at the look on this
blonde's face when she realised that no, in fact
the windows of the new car were NOT tinted —
she was wearing her new sunglasses!

Don't know how we didn't crash!

Transfusion confusion

I was in Beaumont Hospital recently, visiting my Nana who had fallen and broken her hip. There was a really loud guy two beds up from her who had to get blood. The nurse was putting the bag of blood up on the drip and he asked, 'Here, where does this blood come from?'

The nurse replied, 'People donate it.'

The guy says back really loudly, 'Ah right, I thought it was coming from some animal.'

Overheard by Karona, in Beaumont Hospital
Posted on Saturday, 14 April 2007

For the birds

My sister asks my Dad, 'Dad, have you ever seen an owl?'

Quick as a flash my Dad answers, 'An aul' what?'

Overheard by Anonymous, in my Dad's car
Posted on Friday, 13 April 2007

The kids are alright

An old man and woman were talking on the bus about the youth of today. The two of them smelled of booze and it was obvious that they were after having a few drinks. The bloke was giving out about lads and she was giving out about girls.

He says, sounding sad, 'All that these young fellas want to be doing is playing with their Playstations and fighting with knives.'

In a disgusted voice she replies, 'And all the young ones are interested in these days is nightclubs, boozing and the mickey.'

Overheard by I am the resurrection, on the no. 40 bus

Posted on Friday, 13 April 2007

Ulcer says No!

Overheard in a ward in the Mater Hospital the other day.

While visiting my father in a small three-bed ward, man being admonished by his visiting daughter in a broad Dublin accent:

'C'mon, Da, you have to take these tablets, they're for your Ulster!'

Cue stifled giggles as myself and father struggle to compose ourselves and not give the game away.

Overheard by Colm, Mater Hospital

Posted on Thursday, 12 April 2007

Slow Learner

Was getting a lift home with a female friend from college one evening. I noticed that her L plate was on the outside of the windscreen and I asked her why.

She told me 'It was backwards when I bought it, so I had to put it on the outside ...'

Overheard by Kev, front seat of a Nissan Micra

Posted on Wednesday, 11 April 2007

Place your receiver in my USB port

I was working the weekend in a pub in the city centre. The place was surprisingly dead for the bank holiday Monday, only the few auld lads in for the big race at 3.55, the Irish Grand National.

During the build-up to the race, the speakers started acting up and the commentary turned into screeching feed-back, deafening everyone. At which one of the men — true Dub — shouted,

'Whoh, whoh, whoh, jaaaaaysus, f**king turn it down! Sounds like a bloody computer having sex with a telephone ...'

I nearly died laughing!

Overheard by Anonymous, city centre pub
Posted on Tuesday, 10 April 2007

zzzzzzzzzzzzzz

After an extremely dull first 30 minutes at the Ireland v Wales football game in Croke Park, a man a few rows in front of me leaves for the toilet. He passes a man at the end of his row who stands up to let him by, and asks,

'Sorry, did I wake you?'

Everyone around us bursts out laughing!

Overheard by Anonymous, Croke Park, Ireland v Wales
Posted on Monday, 9 April 2007

Smooth

Was out drinking with the mates in Brogan's. A
friend was putting the moves on this girl all
night long, and eventually after a few hours and
a few more drinks it looked like he was in. So he
leans in for the kill when another mate yells
over,

'YOU'RE IN THERE, MATE!'

Instant mood kill — and bloody hilarious!

Overheard by Pól, Brogan's
Posted on Friday, 6 April 2007

Now that's good marketing

Outside the ladies bathroom on the arrivals floor
in Dublin Airport, there's an ad for some
business lounge in the airport or a nearby hotel.

The slogan is, 'Do your business in comfort.'

Genius!

Overheard by Anonymous, Dublin Arport
Posted on Thursday, 5 April 2007

Viniculture

Eating in the posh part of Bon Appetit restaurant
in Malahide. Most of us are so intimidated by the
surroundings that you can hear a pin drop.
Everyone ear-wigging everyone else.

Maître d' asks a gentleman at the next table if Sir
would care to choose wine. Sir asks Maître d' for
a recommendation. Maître d' explains in exotic

(French?) accent that the sommelier will be over shortly and walks off.

Sir's dinner partner asks what Maître d' said. Sir explains that Maître d' didn't know the wines so he's 'sending up a Somalian ...'!

Overheard by Stephen, Malahide
Posted on Thursday, 5 April 2007

It's for me!

My Dad works as a taxi base controller and I was visiting him last night in work. A call came through from a young woman trying to make a booking. When my Dad asked for her address, her reply was, 'It's for me!'

My Dad tried to explain that he needed her address, but she continued to say, 'It's for me in Meath Street!'

My Dad went on to explain that his company does not cover that area and gave her another contact number to call.

This confused young woman said, 'Yes, I called them and told them the taxi is for me but they gave me your number!'

At this stage my Dad was doing his best to hold in the laughter. He advised that he would need an address to secure a booking. The reply he got though was ...

'I don't think you understand, the taxi is for me!'

Overheard by E, taxi base, Clondalkin
Posted on Thursday, 5 April 2007

Hey bud

Walking home alone at the dead of night
through a rough housing estate after a night out,
when an upstairs window swings open.

'Hey, bud,' a voice from the window calls out.

I arch my head to the window and a guy
appears, wearing a vest, and asks, 'Got a smoke?'

I shrugged and answered, 'No.'

Next thing he produces a smoke and asks,

'Got a light?'

Overheard by The rounder, in an unnamed rough neighbourhood
Posted on Wednesday, 4 April 2007

Haggis

In Biology last year, somehow we got onto the
subject of haggis. One of the lads in the class
asked our Scottish teacher (a real joker) what
haggis actually was.

The teacher gave us a load of crap about it being a small animal that lived in the Scottish Highlands which ran around mountains until one leg was shorter than the other (much to the amusement of most of us).

He kept the joke up for about 10 minutes before he put the lad out of his misery and told him the truth. We all laughed about it as the lad looked revolted.

Then five minutes later, one of the less intelligent girls in the class piped up:

'What was the little animal, then, if it wasn't haggis?'

Overheard by CoolKitty, at school
Posted on Wednesday, 4 April 2007

Someone obviously isn't taking honours Maths

A few weeks back, I was travelling on a bus into town when I overheard two guys talking about their Leaving Cert study plans.

'My friend said you're supposed to do 29 and a half hours of study a week.'

'Wow, that's like nearly three hours every day ...'

Overheard by Dave, the bus
Posted on Wednesday, 4 April 2007

More Maths genius ...

In Maths class last week the teacher was giving out homework.

Teacher: 'I want you to do questions nine and ten for homework.'

Girl (blonde hair of course): 'Is dat nine and ten, or nine to ten?'

Overheard by Joey, school
Posted on Tuesday, 3 April 2007

Don't be sorry, Dolly!

At the Dolly Parton gig last night in the Point, Dolly apologised to the people of Cork for the cancelled Millstreet concert at the weekend.

Some voice from the audience pipes up, 'Dolly! It's for the best! They're all a bunch of langers down there!'

Overheard by Anonymous, Point Depot
Posted on Tuesday, 3 April 2007

There's an injured person in trouble somewhere

On the Red Line of the Luas, a Dublin lad gets on with a pair of crutches, both different. Next stop his friend gets on and asks why he's got two different crutches.

'One o' them was robbed off me, so I just went and robbed this one!'

Overheard by Hugh, on the Luas
Posted on Tuesday, 3 April 2007

Leaked email

Bloke I work with was in charge of sending all the emails this morning for late deliveries, apologising to the customers, and he sent out about 50 stating:

'Sorry for any incontinence caused by this delay ...'

One person wrote back saying, 'Thanks for giving the whole office a smile on a Monday morning, but I should probably warn you that there's a big difference between inconvenience and incontinence ... a big difference. Have a nice day.'

He hasn't lived it down!

Overheard by ST, at work
Posted on Monday, 2 April 2007

You want a reason?

Man talking to woman walking through Trinity: 'Cos whenever you get drunk, you get naked!'

Overheard by joetrinners, Trinity College
Posted on Monday, 2 April 2007

Stating the obvious

In my mother's house on Saturday, my Granny, who was staying over for a few days, was on the phone to my Aunty who lives in Canada. The conversation was going on a few minutes when there was obviously some interference on the line.

After a few seconds of Granny repeating my
Aunty's name down the phone and getting no
reply, she turns to me and my old man and says
in all seriousness,

'She seems very far away!'

Overheard by Ted, parents' house
Posted on Monday, 2 April 2007

P45's in the post, pal!

I was working for a car dealer a few years back.
In the valeting department there were two guys
working, Jimmy and new arrival, Simon. Jimmy
was your average middle-aged Dub, tough as old
boots, quick witted and a tongue as slack as a
road worker during rush hour! Simon on the
other hand was Chinese, poor English, timid
and learning the ropes.

They were working away one day when the boss
(who was a real hard ass but had a soft spot for
Jimmy) came strolling along. Immediately, Jimmy
dropped what he was doing and got the boss in
a headlock, and they proceeded to mess fight
with each other. After a few minutes of
handbags, they broke up and the boss walked
away.

Simon, who found this all very amusing on his
first day, gestured towards the Boss and asked
Jimmy, 'Who daaaaa?'

'Whooo him? He's only a little bollix,' and got
back to work.

The next morning Simon was standing in the
showroom outside the boss's office, when in
walks the man himself and walks past Simon.

'How are you?' asks the boss.

Simon turns around and says, 'Hawow littew bowox!'

Overheard by wetblanket, at a car main dealer
Posted on Saturday, 31 March 2007

Beer goggles

A couple of years ago after a christening, my mate was having the afters back in his well-to-do girlfriend's Ma and Da's house. Everybody was having a good time, with the drink flowing. We were all warned to be on our best behaviour and not show him up — all 'please' and 'thank you', and so on.

Our nice but dim buddy, who can't hold his drink, two hours later had to be warned about his behaviour and was told to sit down and chill out. In the lounge were four people including the collared priest who had done the christening that afternoon. He started making polite conversation to my drunk mate, asking what he did for a living, etc.

My mate in a drunken haze replies, 'So, Father, what do you do yourself?'

Overheard by Estaban, first time over in posh Dublin area
Posted on Friday, 30 March 2007

Always keep your eyes on the road!

Was in Blanchardstown last weekend with my sister-in-law. As we walked back to the car park, we noticed this young couple (around 15) kissing by the wall, in clear view of everyone in the multi-storey. All of a sudden this 'boy racer' in a Glanza done up to bits came spinning up on to the level. Just then, all I heard was, 'Getta bleeeeding room!' followed by a big crash …

When we went to investigate closer, this muppet in the Glanza had smacked into the wall, while his head was out the window making smart comments at this lustful couple.

All we could do was laugh … serves him right!!

Overheard by E, shopping in Blanch
Posted on Friday, 30 March 2007

New diagnosis from a taxi driver

Was in a taxi on the way into town last week and had the taxi driver tell me how he was relieved that the clocks were going forward.

He went on to say how he gets depressed during the dark winter months and explained, rather patronisingly, how he was diagnosed as having a relatively unknown disease called 'Mad disease'.

I didn't ask him where the name came from or if he was really a cow, but had to tell him that I thought the name of the disease was SAD (seasonal affective disorder).

Needless to say taxi drivers are never wrong: 'Sure I'm the one sufferin' from it! I should know!'

So after that I had to submit to him that he was right and that correct name for Seasonal Affective Disorder is actually Mad disease.

Overheard by Cossie, taxi
Posted on Friday, 30 March 2007

Lycra ladder

While walking from the bus to college the other week, I was passing by a building which was being renovated. A group of builders stood hanging over the scaffolding.

In front of me there was a woman in her early 20s wearing a denim mini skirt with black tights underneath. As she walked by the builders, the usual whistles started, until one of them shouted, 'You've got a ladder in your tights love!'

In true northside fashion, without even thinking, she spins around and shouts up at him,

'So why don't ya climb up it and kiss my arse!' followed by giving him the finger!

Genius!

Overheard by Dane, D'Olier Street
Posted on Thursday, 29 March 2007

No passport needed

I flew out from London Heathrow (after going through UK customs, getting my picture taken, passport checked about four times and questioned and searched).

Landed in Dublin and made my way to passport control, only to discover I couldn't find my passport. I say to the garda behind the desk that I can't find my passport. He pauses for a minute and asks me where I'm from. I tell him I'm from Dublin, to which he says,

'Ahh, feck it, go on through then.'

Only in Ireland!

Overheard by Fuzzy, Dublin Airport
Posted on Thursday, 29 March 2007

Clap your hands for Jesus

I work as a photographer and was in work one day when this woman brings her kid in to get his photos done. He's sitting there, refusing to smile, and she's trying to get him to clap his hands, which apparently makes him smile, when she comes out with this gem:

'Clap your hands for Jesus! Clap your hands for Jesus — or I'll smack you.'

Overheard by L, in work
Posted on Tuesday, 20 March 2007

Lost

I saw this in the ladies in college some time ago at the top of the door. It said,

'I lost my virginity' and at the bottom it said '... but I still have the box that it came in!'

Overheard by DIZZYDUB, graffiti in the
ladies toilets in Cathal Brugha Street DIT
Posted on Tuesday, 20 March 2007

Dirty minds

In the lift in work the other week, I was going from the ground floor to the fourth floor of the building. A few other people in the lift with me and some from my office. The lift didn't go straight up to where we wanted to go, firstly going to the car park, then stopping again at the ground floor and second floor, letting people in and out.

When the lift stopped again at the third floor, one of the girls from my team turns to me and says,

'Oh my God, it looks like we'll never get back to our desks. I think we're destined to spend the rest of the day riding in the lift.' Cue me and everyone else left in the lift bursting out laughing — and her turning bright red.

Overheard by Johnny, lift in a building in the IFSC
Posted on Tuesday, 20 March 2007

Giz 20 Blue

I was in the Spar the other day buying cigarettes and this kid (no more then 12) comes in, skips the queue, and goes, 'Here, chung one, giz 20 Blue.' The girl at the till goes, 'Do you have ID?' Getting in a right mood, he spits on the ground and goes, 'Do I look like I have any bleedin' ID?'

Overheard by Anonymous, Glasnevin
Posted on Monday, 19 March 2007

Toilet humour

In a pretty run-down gents toilet in Ballyfermot College, I was reading the usual graffiti ('Up the RA', 'Liverpool rule', etc.) in one of the cubicles when I came across this gem:

'Sinead Conway is a ride.'

Directly underneath that:

'No I'm not!'

Overheard by Donall, Ballyfermot College
Posted on Monday, 19 March 2007

Scallops

Standing beside an extremely drunk guy in a Chinese take-away one night I heard him ask about the scallops. It went like this:

Drunk: 'What's no. 15?'

Waiter: 'Is scallops.'

Drunk: 'Yea, but scallops of what?'

Waiter: 'Is scallops, is scallops!'

Drunk: 'Yea ya dope, but scallops of what ... pork, chicken or what?'

Waiter: 'Is scallops, please, is scallops ...'

This went on for about 10 minutes, till the drunk gave in and said:

'Yea, well, I'll have it — but make it a mixture of scallops!'

Overheard by Anonymous, Chinese in Bray
Posted on Monday, 19 March 2007

Stirring the pot

Overheard at the bus stop:

'Bisto are bringing out a new line in honour of our rugby team. It's called "Laughing Stock"!'

Overheard by Anonymous, bus stop, Parkgate Street
Posted on Monday, 19 March 2007

Karma?

I'm walking down Collins Avenue and there's a guy (probably a student) a few paces in front of me, smoking. Group of hoodied 'yung fellas' on bicycles squeeze by me and cycle next to him.

Hoodie: 'Oi mista, can I have a lighter?'

Student: 'Ah ... okay ... here ...'

Hoodie lights his cigarette and starts cycling away with lighter.

Student (somewhat resigned to the fact he's lost it): 'Ah ... you can give me that back now ...'

Hoodie (cycling across road at speed with his mates, laughing obnoxiously): 'Hahaha, ya thick bollix, I said *have* not *borrow* ...'

Right at that moment — as if by divine intervention — Hoodie drops his packet of fags, and they end up crushed under the wheel of his mate's bike.

Overheard by Fred, Collins Avenue by
pedestrian crossing at DCU
Posted on Monday, 19 March 2007

Religion, from a five-year-old's perspective!

Was with my five-year-old nephew and his little friend going for a walk. Little friend kept running ahead. My nephew put up with it for a few minutes, then roared at his friend,

'Bradley, will you stop running out on the road, or we'll end up with a dead body like Jesus!'

Overheard by eimer, small town outside Dublin
Posted on Monday, 19 March 2007

Racist and confused

Was in a chemist in town recently when a young girl tried to walk into the shop. The black security guard quickly stopped her and told her she was barred and not to even think about going in, to which she confidently replied,

'F**K OFF YOU BLEEDIN' CHINK!'

Overheard by Anonymous, Henry Street
Posted on Sunday, 18 March 2007

Product recall!

I nipped out for a sandwich at lunch today. As I was passing by the Specsavers shop on College Green, a guy walked out of the shop. He was looking the opposite way to where he was walking, and barged straight into two builder types on their lunch.

One of the lads says to him, 'Here, Mister, I think you better go back in there and get a stronger pair of glasses — ya lampy bollix!'

Overheard by RonBurgundy, College Green

Posted on Sunday, 18 March 2007

Ignorance breeds contempt

Overheard in Hartigan's, Leeson Street, the night Ireland played Georgia in the Rugby World Cup. A Georgian player was being interviewed in English by RTÉ. Quote random punter:

'That guy works in Spar!'

Overheard by 73man, Hartigan's Pub, Leeson Street

Posted on Sunday, 18 March 2007

Putting your foot in it

In a pretty exclusive golf club in Wicklow a few years back, they held the world amputee championships. My friend was working in the golf shop at the time.

The manager of the shop is a real talker. Loves chatting to people who come into the shop. I used to work there too so I know what he's like.

There's a million and one stories but this one really stands out!

After the event had finished, the world amputee champion came into the shop. General chit-chat for a while, then this guy (American with prosthetic limbs) asked about getting a taxi to the airport.

Without blinking an eyelid or thinking, the manager of the shop replied,

'Ah, you don't want to get a taxi nowadays, sure it'd cost ya an arm and a leg from here!'

The American didn't know what way to take it — and promptly left!

Overheard by Bobby, Wicklow (not Dublin but close)
Posted on Sunday, 18 March 2007

County Cork: a skanger summary

On the no. 39 bus to Blanch. Real Anto and Dermo just behind me.

Anto: 'Stoooory, Dermo, where were ya over the weekend, bud?'

Dermo: 'Ah, I was in Cork, bud.'

Anto: 'Any good, bud?'

Dermo: 'Deadly buzz, man! All the girls are sluts and all the blokes are muppets.'

Overheard by theirishgrover, on the no. 39 bus to
Blanchardstown
Posted on Sunday, 18 March 2007

Randomness

Man on phone: 'Go and ask the back of me flute!'

Overheard by Peter, at a bus stop on O'Connell Street
Posted on Sunday, 18 March 2007

A line to remember

Was standing out in the smoking area of a club one night, minding my own business. A true Dub chanced his arm as he walked past and tried to chat up a foreign girl; she was some sort of European.

After a moment or two, the boyfriend appears, another Dub, and says, 'Here, mate, I hope you're not tryin' to chat my bird up?'

To which the chancer replies, 'It's not your bird, mate, it's just your turn!'

Overheard by Si, Dandelion, St Stephen's Green

Posted on Saturday, 17 March 2007

Horses for courses

Was waiting for a train in Heuston Station last week, and there was a drunk guy pestering people for money. He spotted a very pretty girl, went over to her and said,

'I don't want any money, love, but I wouldn't say no to a ride.' Without batting an eyelid she replied,

'Stick around, there's a train to The Curragh along shortly.'

Overheard by Anonymous, Heuston Station

Posted on Saturday, 17 March 2007

Poultry in motion!

Overheard this slagging match by two skangers:

'I bleedin' wish I was a pigeon and you were a statue.'

'Oh yeah, tell yer aul' one to shave her back next time,' came the reply.

Overheard by Derek, at the back of the no. 27 bus
Posted on Saturday, 17 March 2007

Water and glass not so clear anymore?

Was in the canteen in work with the lads and one of them — we'll call him Karl (because that's his name) — was drinking a glass of water. All of a sudden he flips the glass upside down, spilling water all over the table and our lunches.

J: 'Why in f**k's name did you do that?'

Karl (surprised): 'Awh Jaysus, sorry, boyuz. I wanted to see if there was anything on the bottom of me glass!'

Overheard by Tongue-Bar McGowan, work canteen
Posted on Saturday, 17 March 2007

Amazing sheep!

While travelling to Dublin on the train for the day some years back with a few friends, we happened to pass a golf course. Noticing that there were sheep on the green, my rather dim-witted friend turned to her boyfriend and asked why this was.

Quick as a flash, he retorted that they were, 'trained to pick up the stray golf balls and return them to the club house'.

The rest of us all cracked up, while she responded, 'Really? That's amazing!'

She hasn't lived it down to this day!

Overheard by Anonymous, on the train
Posted on Saturday, 17 March 2007

Dogs' life

I was waiting with my two dogs for my fiancé outside the local Londis. Five scumbags came running down the street towards me; three ran into the shop and started causing hassle with the Polish security guard. One started making racist remarks, another started threatening to stab him and pulled out a rusty nail (I don't know what caused this).

While all of this was going on, the two scumbags outside struck up a conversation with me:

Scumbag: 'Nice dogs, Missus, where d'ya get em?'

Me: 'The Dog Pound.'

Scumbag: 'The Pound? What happened to 'em?'

Me: 'They were abandoned.'

Scumbags: 'Jaysus, some people are awful cruel, what's the world comin' to?'

I wish this were made up!

Overheard by Roisin, at the Londis on Parkgate Street
Posted on Saturday, 17 March 2007

Empty head

Long story short ... Mate A is as thick as a breadboard and he's on holliers. Him and Mate B are chatting up these two English girls in a bar and it goes as follows:

Girl: 'Where are you from?'

Mate B: 'Dublin — capital of Ireland.'

Girl: 'No, it's not!'

Mate B: 'Yeah, it is! Here [to Mate A], where's the capital of Ireland?'

Mate A: 'I dunno!'

Mate B: 'Ye plank! Ye live der!'

Mate A: 'Ahhh, Whitestown!'

Overheard by Steve, pub
Posted on Saturday, 17 March 2007

Bang and the scumbags are gone

On the no. 56a bus a few years ago, upstairs, approaching Cocos, minding my own business when all of a sudden a brick comes smashing through the window.

The driver jams on the brakes, and soon after comes upstairs to ask,

'Did anyone see those unholy bastards?' to which someone quickly replied,

'What channel was it on, bud?'

Everyone who heard it cracked up!

Overheard by peter, the good aul' no. 56a bus
Posted on Saturday, 17 March 2007

Stupid question

Was having dinner in an Italian restaurant recently. I wanted to order what I'd had the night before. The waiter told me twice it was number 39, the chicken dish. Stupidly, I asked what did the chicken come on. He looks at me funny and says, 'A plate ...'

Overheard by DAVE, Little Caesars, off Grafton Street
Posted on Saturday, 17 March 2007

Toilet tennis disappointment

Not technically heard in Dublin, but in a house full of Dubliners one summer in Chicago. Sitting down on their toilet, I see to my left the starting point of what looks like a normal game of toilet tennis. After reading 'Look right,' I turn my head to see scribbled on the opposite wall, 'Toilet tennis has been cancelled due to foot and mouth.'

Quality!

Overheard by Stanny Boy, Chicago
Posted on Friday, 16 March 2007

The unfamiliarities of technology!

On the weekend I was sitting down with my Dad having the aul' relaxing Sunday chat. Anyway, I tried explaining the pros and cons of Limewire to him (as ya do), and with that my Mum goes,

'I don't like you using that thing, Chloe, cuz you can attract viruses to the computer!'

And with that my Dad pipes up,

'Are they contagious?'

Overheard by Chloe, at home
Posted on Friday, 16 March 2007

Amateur spray painter

Seen on wall rather than heard. Young skanger must have been caught in the process, but managed to spray paint 'GRADA SCU'!

Overheard by Anonymous, Tallaght
Posted on Friday, 16 March 2007

North or south — I dunno!

A man walking down the street along beside the DART track, hears a DART going by but could not see it, so he asks a local. The conversation went as follows:

Man: 'Sorry, excuse me ...'

Local: 'Yup.'

Man: 'Did you see that train that went by there?'

Local: 'Yup.'

Man: 'Was it going north bound or south bound?'

Local: 'I dunno, I'm not a bleedin' compass!'

But he found out in the end.

Overheard by Thomas, Seapoint DART station
Posted on Friday, 16 March 2007

Scumbag in training

I saw a small boy about four years old trying to give some skangers in a car the birdie — he stuck up his index finger.

Skangers to boy: 'What's that supposed to mean?' His father then shows him how to do it properly! As the car drives off the boy shouts,

'F**k off, ye bastards,' as his Dad cheers him on.

Overheard by Jono, Finglas
Posted on Friday, 16 March 2007

Famous Dublin landmarks

Two English guys in town, walking along the Quays, just coming up to O'Connell Bridge, obviously trying to find their bearings.

1st Guy: 'Oh look, I remember that bridge there' (pointing at O'Connell Bridge).

2nd Guy: 'Oh yeah, you're right, this is near where Abrakebabra is.'

I just wonder what we're coming to, when Abrakebabra is a more famous Dublin landmark than O'Connell Bridge!

Overheard by Rosi, Aston Quay
Posted on Friday, 16 March 2007

Not so much unheard as unseen!

Advice from the National Consumer Agency to disgruntled holidaymakers:

'Write everything down, keep a record. For example, if there is a problem with the swimming pool — or if there is NO swimming pool as promised — document it with a photograph!'

Overheard by Anonymous, last night's *Evening Herald*
Posted on Friday, 16 March 2007

The pen is mightier than the laptop

Snippet of conversation I overheard ...

Flatmate: 'Well, we'll make a list, then run up to Tesco's and do some shopping.'

His stupid D4 girlfriend: 'Good idea. Hold on ... I'll just get my laptop from my bag. Oh, but I've no printer with me. Do you have a printer?'

Flatmate: 'Uh ... we'll just use a pen.'

Overheard by Fred, in the kitchen
Posted on Thursday, 15 March 2007

Pet name?

On the no. 18 bus a while ago, sitting upstairs, a father was at the very front with his young daughter, around three, sitting beside him, and two other children on the seat across.

He and the youngest were talking to the mother on the speaker phone, and the young girl was shouting down the phone to the mother. The girl said they were at a certain point and everyone on the bus could hear the mother say, 'Okay, I'll see you in a while.'

The husband says goodbye, then the young girl shouts down the phone, 'See you, big tits!'

Overheard by Anonymous, the ever reliable no. 18 bus
Posted on Friday, 16 March 2007

Albert Book, inventor of the novel ...

I was in the basement of Eason's with a mate of mine who was looking for a map of Dublin. While I was wandering around, a gaggle of Three Stripers passed me by. As they passed, one of them said (and I'm quoting his EXACT words heard):

'Sure, what do yez want to buy a book for? Books is the stupidest invention ever!'

Sweet Jesus ...

Overheard by Icecream, Eason's
Posted on Thursday, 15 March 2007